POCKET YOUR PROBLEMS

D1375959

COPING
WITH STRESS

Also available in this series:

POCKET YOUR PROBLEMS

COPING
WITH STRESS

Dr Donald Meichenbaum

Illustrated by Mel Calman

Introduced by
Virginia Ironside of Woman magazine

CENTURY PUBLISHING
LONDON

This book was devised and produced
by Multimedia Publications (UK) Ltd

Editors *Anne Cope and Christopher Fagg*
Design *Mike Spike*
Index *Anne Hardy*

Text copyright © Donald Meichenbaum 1983
Compilation copyright © Multimedia Publications (UK) Ltd 1983
Cartoons copyright © Mel Calman 1983

First published in Great Britain in 1983
by Century Publishing Co. Ltd,
76 Old Compton Street, London W1V 5PA

ISBN 0 7126 0083 3 (paperback)
0 7126 0242 9 (cased)

Printed in Great Britain by
The Anchor Press Ltd, Tiptree, Essex

Contents

Dedication

This book is dedicated to my four children—Lauren, Michelle, David and Danny—who taught me how to cope with stress.

The book was written during a sabbatical leave supported by a Canada Council Fellowship. I am grateful to my wife Marianne and to Myles Genest for their helpful editorial comments.

Introduction

We all know what stress feels like, whether we call it nerves, anxiety, panic, tension, pressure . . . We all get it whether we are driving the car to work, sitting at the playgroup knowing the house is in a mess, presenting reports at board meetings, jetting from Hong Kong to Sydney . . . And the symptoms are exactly the same and just as difficult to cope with whether one is a housewife, a senior executive or a prime minister.

I get thousands of letters from people who are suffering from stress, though sometimes they call their problem something else. They say 'I just can't cope', or 'Things are getting on top of me' or 'I think I'm going mad'. But they are all talking about stress.

Some experiences are hard for anyone to cope with, but it is often those churning inner feelings, not events themselves, that pursue us to breaking point. Otherwise why is it that one woman becomes severely depressed because, say, her son is unemployed, while another sails through life in a golden haze while the bailiffs knock at the door, her husband runs off with his secretary, and her children fall off their motorbikes? Fiddling while Rome burned was probably taking things too far, but Nero would never have broken down just because a guest didn't turn up for dinner.

But a life without stress would be no life at all. Everything in life, especially the crisis points, is potentially stressful. All change is potentially stressful, not only social change like marriage or divorce, but the vaguer changes posed by microchips and stockpiles of nuclear warheads. Nevertheless stress is the spark that pushes us to further our careers, demand better conditions for our children, move house, go on holiday . . . Stress can be the tiny irritant in the oyster that makes the pearl—valuable—or it can be the pinch of salt in the fruit salad—ruinous.

One criticism I usually have of books on stress is that when I am under pressure I am too tensed up to put all those excellent relaxation techniques into practice, even though I know they help. That is why this particular book is so unusual and interesting: it is not a self-help book as such, although it contains many tips and techniques to relieve stress, but a helpful book because it explains what stress actually is and how it occurs.

The more I read about stress the clearer it becomes that many of our reactions to threat are more Pavlovian than rational. Our bodies actually 'learn' to respond to situations stressfully, and the longer we keep up these responses the more ingrained they become, to the point where even a non-event like someone ringing the doorbell becomes the straw that breaks the camel's back. Only by standing back from the situation and analyzing clearly and soberly exactly why we react as we do can we stop the repeated damage to mind and body.

Evolution has equipped us to react to stressful situations physically, with a racing heart and fast breathing; these pump more oxygen into the blood in readiness for fight or flight. We are stuck with those learned responses. Now that we are not obliged to fight or flee we get palpitations at our desks! But what if we could unlearn those responses? What if, instead of letting feelings of panic translate themselves into clammy hands and a racing pulse, we try to make the mind-body feedback loop work to our advantage? It is possible to calm feelings of panic by relaxing physically; equally it is possible to learn new ways of thinking which forestall irrational emotions and the physical havoc they cause.

This is the view taken by Dr Meichenbaum, the author of this book, and the general editor of the *Pocket your Problems* series. He and his colleagues have worked for many years to develop techniques for unlearning stressful behaviour and diverting it into useful and positive channels. Reading his very clear account, with its fascinating studies of groups and individuals, you will almost certainly recognize people you know. But most of all you will recognize yourself.

Virginia Ironside

Author's Preface

Stress is a concept used to explain a number of human experiences, most of them negative. In such varied events as suicide, bereavement, ulcers, high blood pressure and mental illness, the experience of stress is a factor contributing to physical and mental disorders. Magazine readers are provided with self-administered stress tests and are told the likelihood of becoming ill if they score above a certain level (a score of above 100, for instance, means a 60 per cent chance of becoming ill). Those who score high are advised to avoid daily stressful events such as driving in heavy traffic.

Books, television programmes and advertisements bombard us with various ways of combating stress. Physical fitness classes, jogging, yoga sessions, meditation lectures, psychotherapy, vitamins, alcohol and prescription drugs, each of which reflects a view of stress and how to cope, are all increasingly popular. All-inclusive 7–14 day 'anti-stress' programmes are among the attractions that bring many visitors to spas.

But exactly what is the nature of stress and what are its effects? How should we cope with stress? This book is designed to examine these questions critically. The objective is not to provide yet another 'anti-stress' book, nor yet a cookbook on 'how to cope', or a recipe for 'how to live'. There are no panaceas or cure-alls, no formulae for living a stress-free life. Indeed, life would likely prove quite boring if we did not experience stress, for in some instances it may have a positive effect.

The objective of this book is rather to help you to become a better consumer of the 'anti-stress' market.

Along with the other books in this series, it is designed to educate, to challenge and to share the current practical knowledge of what can be done to cope more effectively. Both stress and coping are very complex phenomena, which science does not fully understand. It would be presumptuous for anyone to suggest that there are proven ways of avoiding or reducing stress. Instead, we shall consider the state of the art and what we can derive from it.

1

What is stress?

In a real dark night of the soul, it is always
three o'clock in the morning.

F. SCOTT FITZGERALD (1896–1940)

The word 'stress' is used in many different ways.
Some people define it as a condition of the environment—stress is out there in the social and physical
environment. Thus we speak of stressful environments, of the stress of work, competition and war. In
physiology, we talk of extreme temperatures or sleep
deprivation. The concept of stress as a set of external
forces impinging on the individual is borrowed from
engineering, where the term describes the forces on
an object that produce a strain.

Another view of stress relates to the individual's
response when placed in a challenging or threatening
environment. When, in this context, we speak of the
individual as being 'under stress' or 'stressed', we
describe his or her reaction, both psychological and
physiological, to exposure to the challenging environment. Stress is change provoked within the person.

Thus, on the one hand stress may be viewed in
terms of a set of events that overwhelm the individual,

on the other hand as a set of psychological and physiological reactions. In psychological jargon, stress is equated with the stimulus (input) as well as with the response (output).

Stress and the individual

The transactional view of stress adopted here is one that is being increasingly accepted. Although the term may sound technical, it is relatively simple, and it helps to convey some very important aspects of stress.

The word 'transactional' indicates that stress is influenced both by the individual and by the environment. It is not simply a series of undesirable events *per se* that cause stress, but rather the way a person views such events. Consider, for example, a severe stress situation such as fire, flood or personal mishap. Some individuals experience extreme reactions: they are shaken, stunned and bewildered and experience accompanying bouts of hysterical crying and paralysing anxiety. But others may respond in a cool and collected fashion. There is no predictable pattern of reaction. Each individual helps to define which situations he or she will view as stressful.

There are two important points about the transactional model. First, what is threatening and stressful for me is not necessarily so for you. Some of us endure severe stressful events with style and grace and seem to become stronger with each adversity. Second, we are not mere victims of stress. Indeed, we often behave in ways that help to create, maintain or escalate the stress we experience. There is a dynamic relationship, a transaction, between the individual and the environment which determines what is stressful and how the individual responds; this relationship changes over time.

In short, stress resides neither in the situation nor in the person, but depends on the transaction of the individual in the situation. Let me give you a personal example of what I mean. Most parents will be familiar with the 'instant chaos', about to be described; readers without children can look upon my experiences as a

vicarious trial in stress-inoculation training or as a
form of birth control.

Bad news at bedtime

My wife went out one evening and it was my job to serve dinner and put my four children to bed, a usual occurrence. The regular sequence of events was to tidy up after dinner, give baths, help with homework, read stories and so on. My goal was to complete all this before nine o'clock and then sit back, relax and watch a special television programme.

Everything began well as Danny, my two-year-old, and I thoroughly enjoyed his bath. Lauren (who is ten) was doing her homework and asked if I could help her to find her ruler. To encourage her independence, I asked, 'Where did you last see it?', without searching for it myself. After Danny was in bed, the next task was to see that David (age four) had a bath. Fortunately, Michelle (four years his senior) said that she was going to have a bath and volunteered to bath David at the same time. I readily accepted her help. So far, so good.

While I was cleaning up the kitchen, I could hear David running back and forth in the bath. My head was immediately filled with images of catastrophe—a fall, a split skull, and so on—and I raced up the stairs to stop him. As I opened the bathroom door, the doorknob smashed into Michelle's eye.

Meanwhile, David continued to run in the bath. I yelled at him to stop, trying at the same time not to awake sleeping Danny. My yell startled David and he fell into the water—exactly what I had been trying to avoid! He swallowed some water and began to choke. At this point Lauren innocently arrived on the scene and asked if I had found her ruler yet. 'What? Your ruler!' I exploded. 'Don't you see what has happened? We're in complete chaos and you ask about your ruler!' At this point, she burst into tears and, of course, sleeping Danny now woke up.

All parents have experienced similar incidents, and all have learned to deal with them. I put ice on Michelle's eye, put Danny back to bed, comforted David, and I never did find the ruler for Lauren. By now, it was only just after nine o'clock and I thought I could still see most of my television programme. A glass of Scotch in hand, I collapsed in front of the television, just alert enough to hear Michelle calling for a drink of juice. Feeling very bad about what had happened to her eye, I took a glass of grape juice to her. Yes, she accidentally spilled it all over herself and the bed. As I surveyed this final catastrophe, I kept firmly in mind my resolve not to lose all self-control and hit my children in anger. I felt that I should express my anger, but I did not wish to hit. I also reflected, as philosophically as I could, that at some later time I would read the book on which the television programme was based.

When my wife came home and asked how everything was, I sighed wearily, 'Fine! Someday you'll read about it in a book I write. Right now I don't have the energy to relive it.'

Incidents like these have always made me wonder why the incidence of child abuse is not higher than it is. Not that it is under-reported, but rather how do non-abusing parents cope with frustration and anger? I am reminded of the old adage: 'Insanity is indeed inherited . . . you get it from your children!'

My anecdote illustrates one type of stress: the daily hassles of life. Such insidious sources of stress are pervasive, and each of us develops some means of coping with them. It also illustrates the transactional view of stress.

What is going on?

One can analyse this anecdote at several levels. A central feature in my stressful experience was the variety of my conscious thoughts and images. Consider the impact of the 'catastrophizing' image of David cracking his head open on the bath, or the things I said to myself to control my anger. How I appraised my children's behaviour influenced my reactions. Seeing it as a threat to my authority and as an interruption of my plans had a different impact from considering it as a problem to be solved.

There was more going on cognitively that helped to determine the degree of stress. Various hidden agenda (for example, my desire to watch television) and current concerns (my desire not to hit my children) entered the situation. In addition, a number of implicit beliefs, attitudes and perhaps not readily conscious thoughts about my wife's going out, and feelings about the unceasing demands of being a parent, influenced my degree of stress.

The interruption of my plans had a central role in engendering my stressful reactions. But we often do things that result in frustration and stress, as I did. Putting four children to bed and having a hidden agenda now seems to me to be asking for trouble. By our own actions we often contribute to events that will only interrupt our plans and create stress. How much stress you suffer will be determined by how committed you are to completing your plan and how severe the interruption is. In short, we often contribute to our own demise, although sometimes inadvertently. The idea is central to a transactional model of stress.

Together with these thoughts and feelings came changes in my bodily processes. I felt physically tense; my breathing became deeper and faster, my heart-rate accelerated, my blood pressure rose. Although I was unaware of it, at the biochemical level changes in both hormones and enzymes were accompanying my stress. Research has indicated that over 30 different hormones are set into motion when individuals are stressed.

Finally, one additional influence was knowing that my wife would return home soon. Knowing that help was on the way, and that the stress would run its course and end, lessened my reactions. I also knew that I could tell my wife, tongue-in-cheek, what *her* kids had done to me!

Such anecdotes may help us to understand better why the incidence of child abuse is highest in single-parent families. Imagine the burden of having to meet all the demands of life and, in addition, cope with the stress of parenting. Some of you will no doubt not have to 'imagine' but will know all too well from personal experience.

The last thing
I want to know
is that 30 different
hormones are activated
when I feel stressed!

Sources of stress

The way you interpret a situation determines whether it will produce a stress response, and the way you behave can create, maintain or escalate the stress. Stress is a by-product of the transaction between the individual and the environment.

Putting four children to bed is only one of the many sources of stress best described as daily hassles— stable, repetitive problems encountered in everyday life. Usually, they do not present great demands, nor is much effort required to cope with them. However, in some conditions, they may become chronic and take their toll. The gradual build-up of relatively insignificant events can prove more devastating than a single traumatic event.

Job dissatisfaction, crowding and commuting may all contribute to stress. On-the-job stress, for instance, may have a number of causes. The job may require a great deal of effort and rapid decision-making; or its requirements may be complex or ambiguous; or there may be the threat of unemployment, pressure for advancement, job role conflict, or pressures to conform. Unsatisfactory work conditions, including repetitive, boring work, inconsiderate supervisors, rotating shifts and so forth call for coping responses. Because the daily hassles are regular and permanent, you may not realize how severe they are, but in the long run they may require more effort at adjustment than other causes of stress.

Traumatic or cataclysmic events are a second source of stress. Natural disasters (floods, earthquakes) or man-made ones (violence, accidents, fires, etc.) are sudden, unique and powerful events that often affect large groups of people, while illness, death or major loss are equally traumatic although they affect fewer people. Loss is another major source of stress: the death of your spouse, child, friend; a divorce; a love affair that goes hopelessly wrong; or the loss of an important source of reward, such as a job. Let us consider the impact of some of these events.

Disaster at Buffalo Creek

On 26 February 1972, a slag dam collapsed, inundating the valley of Buffalo Creek, West Virginia. The churning black mud and water carried with it bridges, houses, cars and human bodies. In their work on the impact and aftermath of the disaster, Goldine Gleser,

Bonnie Green and Carolyn Winget reported that: 'People who had scrambled up hillsides to safety watched helplessly as relatives, friends, and neighbors were propelled past them by the black swirling waters. Three hours later, the last of the water emptied into the Guyandotte River, leaving 125 dead, many hundreds injured, and thousands homeless.'

The disaster was exacerbated, because the mineowners who controlled the dam were held responsible for the disaster owing to their negligence. In July 1974, they made an out-of-court settlement of $13·5 million, including an unprecedented $3 million for psychological impairment resulting from the disaster. But what exactly was the nature of the impairment and what effect did such traumatic events have?

The victims of the Buffalo Creek disaster displayed substantial 'anxiety, depression, somatic concerns, belligerence, agitation, social isolation, and changes in their daily routine and leisure-time activities, and there was considerable alcohol abuse among the males.' Moreover, the extent and duration of these symptoms were not influenced by the fact that a lawsuit against the mine-owners was pending. In fact, those who were not pressing lawsuits suffered more symptoms than those who were.

These patterns of symptoms were evident for two years. At least 35 per cent of the victims were moderately to severely disturbed, despite the helpful efforts of physicians, mental health workers, and religious counsellors. Only one in six adult victims was free of symptoms and, as long as four to five years after the disaster, over 30 per cent continued to suffer debilitating symptoms. At the two-year follow-up assessment, 75 per cent of those interviewed reported difficulty in getting to sleep or staying asleep, and two-thirds reported nightmares involving water and death.

Are these results unique to the Buffalo Creek disaster, or do other victims of traumatic stressful events react so severely? It is difficult to know, because there have been too few adequate long-term studies of the victims of natural disasters and, in such studies as have been conducted, different types of measure (interviews, surveys, questionnaires) have been used and different criteria of adjustment have been employed. At the moment, all we can conclude is that all disasters are not equivalent in terms of the stress they produce. Such factors as the scope or impact of the disaster (how large an area and how many people are involved); the speed of onset (sudden, gradual, chronic); the duration of impact; and the community's preparedness for the disaster all influence the nature of the victims' reactions.

In terms of each of these factors, the Buffalo Creek disaster was quite severe, which may help to account for the large incidence of psychological symptoms.

The disaster threatened the lives of most of the community and left them bereaved. Although the disaster was sudden, its consequences lasted quite a long time, and the victims felt an accompanying sense of betrayal towards the mine-owners.

It is important to appreciate, however, that not all disasters lead to such widespread and long-lasting psychological distress; nor do all victims suffer to the same degree. Our resilience or ability to cope plays an important role in determining how we respond to such traumatic events. Our philosophy of life, expectations, self-confidence, range of coping skills, and the amount of help we get from others, all influence resilience.

Adapting to another culture

Another form of stressful experience is something known as 'acculturation'. The word describes the process by which communities and people adjust to the stress of major changes that accompany exposure to the values or life style of another culture. Loss of one's culture, or its absorption by another, is an increasing source of stress.

Consider the following example offered by Gottlieb Guntern. He studied what happened to the people of the isolated village of Saas Fee in the Swiss Alps as it was transformed virtually overnight into a famous, affluent tourist resort from a rural farming community after a road was opened in 1957. By 1970, over 250 000 winter tourists and 500 000 summer tourists were invading this previously secluded area, producing a ten-month tourist season when villagers had to work long hours each day, seven days a week. What impact did loss of their life style have on the villagers?

As the economy developed, major role changes took place. Family ties and parental involvement in raising children weakened, and the importance of the peer group increased. The children of Saas Fee began to take on some of the attributes and habits of the visitors (e.g., language, walk, use of alcohol and drugs). The gap between younger and older generations increased. Not only children were affected. Rapid social change took its toll of adults, producing chronic fatigue, irritability, insomnia and various psychophysiological disorders, including ulcers, headaches, high blood pressure. Alcoholism also increased, especially among the young and women, hard liquor replacing wine. The community also became less tolerant towards mentally ill people, because of a desire to maintain the peace and satisfaction of the guests.

Life events which cause stress

Natural calamities such as the Buffalo Creek disaster and the pressures of living in a new environment are only two of many possible stressful events. Table A shows a very wide variety of different 'stresses', or stress events. Such life events are a continuing source of stress to which we are all subject, to a greater or lesser extent. They vary in a number of ways. They may differ in their importance to the individual

---

Table A
Examples of life stress events

Death of spouse
Death of close family member or friend
Major personal illness or injury
Serious illness or injury of close family member
Major change in closeness of family members
Engagement
Marriage
Marital separation (owing to conflict)
Divorce
Trouble with in-laws
Son or daughter leaving home
Gaining a new family member
Major change in financial status
Foreclosure on mortgage or loan
Borrowing money
Changed work situation (conditions, hours, amount of responsibility)
Trouble with employer
New job
Being made redundant
Retirement from work
Change of residence
Major change in living conditions of family
Minor violations of the law

---

concerned; in their duration, severity and predictability; in the suddenness of their onset; and in the degree of control and self-confidence with which we deal with them. Sometimes the changes they represent are minor, at other times severe and clearly threatening. We not only react to dangers or threats that have already materialized, we are equally affected by the expectation that those events will occur.

Responding to stress

Stress events usually lead to a call for action, accompanied by uncertainty about the appropriate response and its outcome. The stress event implies a significant change. The person experiencing the stress may feel overwhelmed, anxious, unhappy, depressed, hopeless and helpless. Such feelings arise from comparing perceived demands and one's ability to cope. An imbalance in this coping process, when coping is important, leads to the experience of stress.

Table A shows that stress is a fact of life. We cannot eliminate it—nor would this be desirable. Given the ubiquitous nature of stress, the key is our ability to cope with stress; we are distinguished not by the stress we experience, but by how we cope with it.

Good stress?

Although many of us seek to avoid stress, others eagerly seek the challenge and joy of confronting and mastering stressful events, either as part of our daily routine or in recreation. In his book, *Stress Without Distress*, Hans Selye, a Canadian endocrinologist who developed the concept of stress, recognizes its potentially positive aspects. Selye distinguishes between the stress of failure or frustration, which is harmful ('distress'), and other kinds of stress, such as challenges, which he sees as benign or even beneficial ('eu-stress'). He notes that life is most interesting and comfortable when we have enough stress to give it

If you men weren't so BORING — you'd go and get some STRESS in your lives...

excitement, but not so much as to cause distress. Too little stress can lead to a boring, joyless existence.

Consider the following accounts, which describe how some people seek stressful events. First, Chris Bonnington, the famous British mountaineer, writes of the stress and the joy of climbing:

> 'At the start of any big climb I feel afraid, and dread the discomfort and danger I shall have to undergo. It's like standing on the edge of a cold swimming-pool trying to nerve yourself to take the plunge; yet once in, it's not nearly as bad as you have feared; in fact it's enjoyable.
>
> Once I start climbing, all my misgivings are forgotten. The very harshness of the surroundings, the treacherous layers covering every hold, even the high-pitched whine of falling stones, all help build up the tension and excitement that are ingredients of mountaineering.'

The following accounts come from interviews with a group of surgeons:

> 'You become quite tense, pulse goes up, may be sweaty. The key to a good surgeon is one who is cool and can get out. Requires skill. He must keep calm and analyze the problem. Your reaction depends on how serious you think the problem is.'

'I get mad at myself, and think that I'm a stupid SOB, then I correct it, calmly.'

'You get upset, but try to solve the problem. You have to keep going because of the seriousness. Outside of the operating room you might scream and shout if something goes wrong—but not while operating.'

'If things go wrong you may feel dreadful later, but at the time you just repair it. It is a logical, technical problem—no reason to panic or lose one's temper.'

It is not events themselves but how we view them and how we cope that determine the nature of stress. Challenge and thrill are as much a part of stress as conflict, threat and anxiety, but each leads to different appraisals of what to do. Perhaps the Chinese understand the appraisal process best. In Chinese, the word 'crisis' combines the symbols for the words 'danger' and 'opportunity'. What happens will largely be influenced by how we view the stress event and by our ability to cope.

REMEMBER—
In Chinese
the word 'CRISIS'
combines the words
'danger' and 'opportunity'...

... I'm very happy for them...

2

The appraisal process and stress

Oh the nerves, the nerves; the mysteries of this machine called man! Oh the little that unhinges it: poor creatures that we are!

CHARLES DICKENS (1812–1870)

Picture two colleagues, both with essentially the same speaking skills, who are asked to speak in public. Colleague A has been anxious when speaking in front of a group for as long as he can remember. Some of his worst memories from school are of fumbling for words in front of a tittering class. Since then, he has deliberately tried to improve his speaking skills, and he is now a reasonable speaker, even though his anxiety in such situations has remained high. Colleague B, by contrast, does not usually find that public speaking makes her particularly anxious, although her speaking skills are similar to those of her colleague.

During each speech, some members of the audience walk out of the room—an exodus viewed in quite different ways by the two individuals.

Colleague A says to himself: 'I must be boring. How much longer do I have to speak? I never could give a speech. I'm making a fool of myself.' These thoughts not only arise from his anxiety, they engender yet more anxiety. They also become self-fulfilling prophecies: his speech deteriorates as he becomes more and more anxious, and the deterioration confirms his previous thoughts.

Colleague B views the audience's departure as a sign of rudeness or attributes it to external circumstances. She says to herself: 'They must have to go somewhere. Too bad they have to leave; they will miss hearing me.'

Exams: the pressure to perform

A similar pattern of different thinking styles is also evident among people with high and low test-anxiety. For instance, imagine an exam in which some students hand in their papers early. In the high test-anxiety student, who is still working away, this event elicits worried self-statements such as 'I don't understand this problem. I'll never finish. How can they have finished?' which lead in turn to increased anxiety and further irrelevant and self-defeating thoughts. In comparison, the low test-anxiety student readily dismisses the other student's performance, saying: 'Anyone who hands in papers early must be doing pretty badly.'

Thus both the high speech-anxiety and the high test-anxiety individuals focus their attention on themselves and personalize the situations and challenges with which they are confronted. The low speech- and test-anxiety individuals, on the other hand, plunge into a task when being evaluated. The same stimulus events are viewed differently and result in different reactions. How we react to events goes a long way towards determining whether they are viewed as personal threats or challenges.

Coping and personal attitudes

Another set of examples will show you how the views people take of situations do much to determine the nature and impact of stressful events. Ronnie Janoff-

Bulman and Camille Wortman, two Chicago psychologists, interviewed 29 people paralysed in serious accidents in order to determine how well they were coping with the stress of a sudden mishap (e.g., an automobile accident, a fall down stairs, a diving or football injury). People were described as coping well if they had accepted the reality of their injury and were attempting to deal positively with the paralysis. They were considered to be coping poorly if they denied the extent of their injuries despite medical evidence to the contrary; if they denied the amount of rehabilitation needed; if they expected to get better 'miraculously'; or if they showed no interest in improving their condition or attending physical therapy sessions.

The interviews revealed that how individuals thought and felt had a marked influence on the coping process. Some victims took the attitude that their fate had been determined by others. They resented other people, felt helpless and were unable to develop a sense of control towards the future. The more these victims seemed to blame others for the accident, the worse they coped.

By contrast, victims prepared to accept some blame for their injuries were able to find a more adaptive response. Those who felt responsible for their accident also felt responsible for their recovery. There was less of a tendency among these people to become dependent and apathetic. In fact, a number of patients even managed to evaluate their disability positively. These patients were able to find positive features in stressful experiences while they were enduring them. For example, one paralysed patient remarked:

> 'It may have been for the best—somebody might have made sure the situation could have been different . . . like I might have died.'

Another said:

> 'Since the accident, I've learned an awful lot about myself and other people. You meet difficult people in a hard-up situation that I never would have met . . . I see the accident as the best thing that could have happened

'cause I was forced to decide my faith, whereas there would have been the possibility that I would have lived and never made a decision—been lost the rest of my life.'

So severe stress such as an accident or disease may not always bring about a crisis. Indeed, such unfortunate occurrences may actually help to solve some people's problems. For example, in some cases disease provides individuals with a welcome relief from the stress of obligations and responsibilities. In other cases, having an unfortunate accident may be viewed by the victim as an occasion to pause and reflect on his or her life style. And so, each of us has the ability to find meaning even in the worst situations. And the nature of the meaning we discover will help to determine how stressed we become.

Rape: interpreting the experience

The role of an individual's thoughts and feelings in the coping process was further illuminated in a second study by Janoff-Bulman, in which she examined the reactions of female rape victims. Just imagine the horror, the stress that accompany violent physical and psychological assault. How do people react and how do their reactions relate to their ability to cope? Janoff-Bulman was able to distinguish two types of reactions that frequently follow such traumatic events. One type can be described as self-blame; the victim attempts to cope with the rape by viewing the incident as a result of something she did or failed to do. For example, some rape victims said:

'I shouldn't have let someone I didn't know into the house.'
'I shouldn't have been out that late.'
'I should not have walked alone.'
'I should not have hitch-hiked.'
'I should not have gone into his apartment.'

What is important to recognize about these reactions is that in each case the woman attributes the cause of the rape to something she did or failed to do, to some behavioural error. To adopt such an explanation may be an adaptive reaction, for it suggests that rape is potentially avoidable. As Janoff-Bulman suggests, rather than being regarded as self-denigrating put-downs, these reactions can be perceived as attempts to re-establish personal control.

In looking at these reactions, it should be emphasized that most rape attacks are not a result of the negligence or carelessness of women. In fact, a recent report concluded that only about 4 per cent of all rape incidents are precipitated by the victim.

Often, rape victims responded with a different set of reactions, called 'characterological self-blame', the tendency to attribute the rape to some character trait or personality flaw they believe they have. Examples of characterological self-blame included:

'I'm too trusting.'
'I'm a weak person.'
'I'm too naive and gullible.'
'I'm the kind of person who attracts trouble.'
'I'm not a very aware person.'
'I'm not at all assertive—I can't say no.'
'I'm immature and can't take care of myself.'

In short, it is not merely being a victim, but how one views and explains the attacks that influences the ability to cope. How the rape victim herself and members of society view the situation plays an important role in how victims adjust. This is not to negate the horror, the terror, the stress of the rape incident itself, but rather to emphasize that reactions to such incidents play a central role in the coping process. By focusing on those aspects of the rape that were alterable, rather than on the relatively non-modifiable aspects, rape victims increased their sense that such negative events could be avoided in the future.

Recognizing threat
In summary, the individual plays a critical role in defining how stressful a set of events is. Individuals'

What is STRESS?
How do we recognise it?
Is it an ILLNESS?
Is it a symptom of
a greater unease?
Is it?

It's a STRONG
desire to
throttle people
like you...

perceptions, both of the stressfulness of the event and of their ability to cope with it, ultimately define the stress. A situation such as taking an examination can be stressful for one individual, because the exam is perceived as making demands which it might be difficult to meet, whereas it is not stressful for another who does not perceive it thus. Notice that such perceptions may be realistic: that is, the high test-anxiety person may in fact not know the material. Under other circumstances, both the high and low test-anxiety individuals may have approximately equal ability, but may simply evaluate the situation differently. Stress is not simply a result of lack of knowledge, but of an individual's appraisal that he or she lacks knowledge—whether that appraisal is true or not. In the case of the speech-anxiety individual, different previous experiences led to the speakers perceiving their ability to meet the demands of the situation to different degrees.

The example of the test situation also indicates that stress occurs mainly in situations in which the outcome is important to the individual. Failing an exam or bungling a speech usually matters quite a lot.

Minor failures are less likely to be associated with stress.

It is not the nature of the stress event itself but our psychological perception of the implied threat that influences how we react. To bring the point home, imagine someone who has had a very serious car accident. Research has indicated that whether the victim is conscious or unconscious (that is, whether he or she is aware or unaware of the severity of the injuries) is critical in determining how the body reacts. Autopsies showed that only in those who had been conscious of their situation were the biochemical bodily changes that signify stress visible. Those victims who had remained unconscious before death showed no stress-like bodily changes. The recognition of threat, the perception of stress, seems to be a critical factor in influencing how we respond. It is the psychological significance of the injury, rather than merely the physiological insult, that produces stress. In some important sense, stress is in the eye of the beholder!

Appraising stress

The psychologist Richard Lazarus's description of the appraisal process has helped to define the importance of the perception of stress. The term 'cognitive appraisal' refers to an individual's judgement of the demands and constraints of situations and of the options and resources for meeting them. How we evaluate a transaction with the environment (for example, how I viewed putting my four children to bed) reflects the appraisal process.

Appraisal: a two-tier process

Lazarus has defined two main kinds of appraisal—primary and secondary. By primary appraisal is meant the judgement that the situation is relevant or irrelevant, a challenge or threat, potentially beneficial or harmful. Such judgements are made at an automatic or unconscious level. In short, primary appraisal answers the question 'Am I OK or in trouble?' It evaluates what is at stake. Whether we view an event as a threat, a potential loss or a challenge will determine the degree of the stress reaction. Our beliefs, values, goals and commitments influence our primary appraisal of events.

Secondary appraisal refers to the judgement about the adequacy of the forms of coping available for mastering the demands of a specific situation. It answers the question 'What can I do about the stress?' Secondary appraisal involves evaluating coping strategies in terms of their cost and the probability of their success. How successful the individual has been in the past in such situations, how generally self-confident he or she is, and the material resources available, will all influence the secondary appraisal process. Secondary appraisal, like primary appraisal, occurs automatically. Since our attempts to cope often change the situation, a further reappraisal is required, and so the process continues.

The appraisal process reveals that stress may occur when a demand threatens to exceed an individual's capabilities and resources. The individual's perception of the stressfulness of the event, his perception of his ability to cope with it, ultimately defines the stress.

Stress-engendering thoughts

To illustrate how our thoughts can engender stress, let us look again at the thinking processes of the high test-anxiety and speech-anxiety individuals. Research into individuals who are highly anxious in evaluative situations and who perform poorly while stressed indicates that their thinking processes often have some of the following characteristics:

(a) worry about performance, including how well others are doing compared with oneself;

(b) ruminating too long and fruitlessly over alternative ways of behaving;

(c) preoccupation with bodily reactions (sweaty palms, increased heart rate, heavy breathing etc.);

(d) ruminating about: the possible consequences of performing badly; social disapproval; loss of status or esteem; punishment; damage to one's self-concept;

(e) thoughts and feelings of inadequacy, including active self-criticism or self-condemnation; considering oneself as worthless and helpless and the situation as hopeless.

Images of self-doubt

Thinking that focuses on oneself seems to have an automatic 'run-on' character that produces upsetting feelings and impairs performance by diverting attention from the task in hand to self-evaluative concerns. Thinking that serves to inhibit motivation tends to be negative rather than positive.

Such negative thinking is not limited to anxious individuals making a speech or taking a test. One interesting study examined athletes trying for selection for the US Olympic gymnastics team. The researchers interviewed and gave questionnaires to the athletes before, during and after the competition. They found that those athletes who made the team were distinguished much more by their thoughts and feelings (i.e., their self-verbalizations and images) than by their physical abilities. The successful gymnasts tended to be more self-confident and to use their anxiety and arousal as a stimulant or cue for better performance. Their less successful competitors seemed to arouse themselves into a state of near panic by self-verbalizations and images of self-doubt and impending tragedies.

Similar patterns of debilitating thought processes have been found to contribute to stress in such varied groups as patients undergoing surgery, individuals enduring pain, students trying to be creative in an

I think that I think too much-
I should do LESS thinking-
If only I could STOP ALL THIS THINKING, I'd be much happier...
(I think)

exam, parents handling non-compliant children, and individuals in situations that require assertive behaviour.

Magnifying inadequacy

People who judge themselves unable to cope with stress tend to engage in frequent self-appraisals of their inadequacy, and often consider threats to be more formidable than they really are. They not only magnify the severity of possible threats but worry about perils that rarely—if ever—happen. A vicious circle ensues, whereby such thoughts result in increased bodily reactions, which in turn heighten a preoccupation with inefficiency and potential calamities. For those individuals who doubt their ability to cope, anxious anticipation becomes a preoccupation that often far exceeds the objective hazards and revolves around imagined dreadful social catastrophes.

Once people perceive a situation as very stressful or burdensome, they almost always react to it in a way that tends to increase their feelings of anxiety, anger or despair. People not only think; they also think about their thinking and their feelings, and thereby an individual over-reacts. This reaction, this berating and condemning of oneself for one's poor reaction to stress, exacerbates the stress response yet more. This is the process of 'awfulizing'—responding to situations with thoughts such as 'I should', 'I must', 'I have to do certain things' and 'If I don't do them then how awful it would be', 'How worthless I would be', and so on. Such thoughts interfere with the coping process. It is not merely the reactions one has in a stressful situation—be they anxiety, anger, depression—but also what one says to oneself and feels that determines the nature and duration of the stress response and the adequacy of the coping process.

Discovering alternative meanings

A useful way of thinking about all these factors is to say that each of us has a 'hidden agenda'—a collection of current concerns, worries, uncertainties, priorities and goals which are not necessarily felt consciously. They surface in the way we interpret experience and the overall meaning we attach to situations. They determine whether we will participate, what aspects of the situation we attend and respond to, how intense our involvement will be, and the general level of stress we experience. If we want to change the ways in which situations affect us, we must learn to change our interpretation of them. This is easier to say than to do. But it is helpful to remember, in moments of stress, that solid research has shown that our reactions are *not* the only possible interpretations. There *are* alternatives. And if we can discover these alternatives, not only will we suffer less, but we will be freed to play a more positive role based on our strengths rather than our weaknesses.

3

How stress affects us

Who, except the gods, can live time through
forever without pain?

AESCHYLUS (525–456 BC)

At the subjective level, one may feel at the 'end of one's tether', or 'the pressure of living' may be too much. Our tolerance of stressful situations (frustrations, interruptions, disappointments, and so forth) may be shorter than usual. We may feel restless, tense, irritable, anxious or depressed. We may suffer from loss of appetite, disturbed sleep or insomnia, repetitive nightmares, extensive fatigue, irritability, impaired concentration and memory, withdrawal from social contact, loss of sexual potency and excessive use of alcohol and drugs. We may have many physical complaints and symptoms, and a low resistance to physical illness. Unusual perspiration, swollen ankles, shaky stomach, dry mouth and lips, faster heart-beat and climbing blood pressure are all warning signs that we are under pressure and that it is time to try to cope with stress.

The results of severe stress or prolonged repetitive stress (e.g. daily hassles) may include more serious

bodily disorders such as headaches, high blood pressure, ulcers and other serious illnesses, even death. In short, stress has an impact on our thoughts, feelings, behaviour and physiology.

How the body responds

Bodily signs of arousal, tenseness and biochemical changes do not in and of themselves constitute stress, nor do they always have debilitating effects. The athlete preparing for competition, the astronaut waiting for take-off, the sky-diver about to jump from an aeroplane often show physical and biochemical stress reactions similar to those in people undergoing negative stressful events. A standard laboratory method of stressing someone is to plunge his (or her) hand into a bucket of icy water. While this sounds unpleasant, remember that, each January, members of various Polar Bear clubs take pleasure in swimming in frigid waters.

More is involved in stress than mere exposure to a stressful event. It is not the physiological arousal itself that determines the stress but how one perceives it and what one says to oneself about that arousal. The nature of the individual's appraisal will determine whether the arousal experienced results in debilitating anxiety, paralysing fear or merely eagerness to demonstrate one's competence. Physiologically, these may appear to be the same phenomena, but psychologically they are quite different.

When life events are seen as stressful, they take their toll. We pay for the 'wear and tear' on our bodies generated by repeated and prolonged stress. Situations such as personal threat, prolonged work on monotonous tasks, an overload on a task, loss of control, and unpredictability have each been linked to important bodily changes.

Stress and disease

During the 1970s, there was considerable research into the relationship between stress and disease, in particular into the relationship between stress and cancer, heart disease, tuberculosis, ulcers, hypertension (high blood pressure), skin disorders and asthma. It has been estimated that stress-related disorders such as tension headaches affect about 15 million Americans, while hypertension affects 20 million. Stress takes an equal toll in emotional and mental disorders.

Two general approaches have been used to examine the relationship between stress and illness. In one, the relationship between the occurrence of general life stress events and the *individual's* susceptibility to illness has been studied. In the other, the incidence of illness in a *group* under severe stress is examined and compared with that in a group that does not experience such severe stress. Let's briefly look at both sets of findings.

Whether they are positive or negative, the life stress events listed at the end of Chapter 1 all challenge people's ability to cope and demand readjustment or

A person at the end of their tether ...

reorganization of a person's life. The item consistently considered to require the greatest adjustment is 'death of a spouse'. Next most severe are 'divorce' and 'marital separation'. In terms of subjective feelings of distress, too, the most upsetting events involve the loss of support of a marital partner. What impact do the changes brought about by such events have on physical and mental well-being?

The general finding is that the more life stress events to which an individual has been recently exposed, the greater the likelihood that he or she will contract some form of illness. While the relationship between stress and illness is positive, however, it has not been found to be strong. What this means is that many people who become ill have not suffered a major life event and that many people facing stressful life events do not become ill. The factors that cause illness are far wider than exposure to life stress events alone. One study found that 'hardy' persons who believe they can control or influence events, who feel deeply involved or committed to the activities of their lives, and who anticipate change as an exciting challenge to further development, thrive on a stressful life and cope adequately. They do not become ill.

Where a positive relationship between stressful life events and illness has been shown, it is not specific to any one disease but is related to many disorders, including heart disease, depression and suicide attempts. At worst, exposure to a number of stressful life events may serve to increase one's overall susceptibility to illness, possibly because they are likely to disrupt an individual's everyday activities, whether social activities, eating and sleep habits, or simply the general routine of self-care.

Job-related stress

Studies of particular occupational groups who work in conditions of high stress indicate that stress can take a heavy toll of health. For example, air-traffic controllers shoulder considerable responsibility, a heavy workload, and, in some airports, long stretches of boredom during periods of low activity, all of which contribute to job-related stress. Their job often requires continuous attention, and rapid decisions based on low-quality information—decisions in which errors can be literally catastrophic. One study compared the incidence of various illnesses in two groups, one of air-traffic controllers, the other of airmen. Hypertension was found to be four times as prevalent among the controllers as among the airmen, and the incidence of diabetes and peptic ulcers was about twice as high.

Imagine yourself, for a moment, as an air-traffic controller, making difficult decisions under a great deal of pressure. Each decision has life-threatening implications. You are well trained for the job and you have made such decisions many times in the past. The routine itself seems to help to reduce the stress, yet the stress may accumulate and it can take its toll of the more vulnerable. Now, on top of all this job-related stress, imagine yourself in the position of the air-traffic controllers in the USA who recently had the additional stress of deciding whether to strike. Should you stand up for your rights? Should you defy authority? Should you back your buddies? Should you jeopardize seniority and security and risk unemployment and a questionable future under uncertain economic conditions? Consider the stress this group of men and women experienced. Only future research will help us appreciate the full toll of this tragic set of events.

In another study, a quite different occupational group manifested the ill-effects of a different variety of stress. Among Australian telegraphists, a high incidence of neurosis and psychosomatic disorders (e.g., peptic ulcers, eczema, asthma) was evident in comparison with engineers and clerks. The telegraphists' work was described as monotonous, repetitive, machine-paced, requiring high skill, yet carried out in noisy conditions.

Often the physical and mental impact of stress is cumulative. You can see the cumulative impact of stress on health by looking at a study of the Space Center at Cape Kennedy during the last years of the United States' moon programme. Its workers were faced with an interesting paradox. Each successful mission, culminating in putting a man on the moon, brought the discontinuation of the space project closer, and, besides the stress of accomplishing the missions successfully, there was thus the additional stress of possible future unemployment. As pressure mounted to complete the programme, alcoholism and divorce increased. In addition, the number of deaths among the workers, who were relatively young, suddenly increased, presumably because of heart failure, reaching a peak as the programme was phased out. Several other studies have also indicated the detrimental impact of stressful jobs on physical and mental health.

The link between stress and physical illness

The question now is what factors link stressful job-related activities and physical illness? Research by Marianne Frankenhaeuser at the Stress Institute in Stockholm into biochemical changes in workers in response to stress sheds some light on this problem. She reported that the speed with which individuals 'unwind' after stressful transactions influences the total 'wearing' of the body. Individuals who quickly returned to a physiological baseline in terms of biochemical changes (adrenaline increases and decreases) after being stressed tended to be better balanced psychologically and more efficient achievers than those who returned to the baseline slowly.

In short, it is not mere exposure to job stress, but how the individual responds, how quickly he or she can 'unwind' that determines the physical and bodily toll. Not all air traffic controllers or telegraph operators become ill as a result of work-related stress.

So how do workers unwind? In a study by Dewe, Guest and Williams, middle managers in a transport

industry were asked two questions: (1) can you think of a particular time at work when you felt under stress?; and (2) can you tell me what happened and how you managed to cope with it? On the basis of the answers to these questions, they identified four styles of avoiding, coping and unwinding from stress.

The first style reflected task-oriented coping behaviours. Included in this category were such activities as (a) analysing and getting rid of the causes of stress ('find out more about the situation', 'take immediate action', 'set priorities'); (b) taking actions to avoid and reduce panic ('tackle routine work to get composure back', 'try not to worry', 'try to reassure yourself', 'take a break and come back to it later', 'see the humour in the situation'); (c) taking actions to prevent subsequent repercussions ('let people know where you stand', 'make sure people are aware of what you are doing', 'follow proper channels to cover yourself').

A second coping style focused on the expression of feelings coupled with a search for social support at work. Such coping skills included letting off steam, getting rid of tension by expressing irritability and frustration, removing oneself temporarily from the stressful situation and seeking advice from others.

The third major way in which employees coped with work-related stress was to engage in outside activities such as physical exercise, hobbies and family life, as well as talking over the problem at home away from the stressful environment.

The final coping style involved a passive attempt to ride out the situation, to ignore the sources of stress for the time being. Such statements as 'let the feeling wear off', 'drop what you are doing and take up something totally unrelated', 'move on to something you can get satisfaction from', 'do nothing' and 'try to carry on as usual' illustrate this coping style.

Combining coping styles

While we may tend to use one of these four responses more than others, we often combine various responses (direct action, social support, emotional control). The combination which works best depends upon a number of factors (e.g., the nature of the job, the setting, the attitude of employers, etc.).

Inability to relax after work, job dissatisfaction, absenteeism and psychosomatic symptoms were also found in a group of Swedish sawmill operators. Their working environment had a high degree of stress, and they reported feelings of monotony, non-participation and coercion. The work was machine-paced, requiring rapid, accurate and repetitive decisions in a saw-house with a high level of noise. Moreover, they worked on a shift basis, which meant frequent changes in their sleep cycle, and they were paid on a piecework basis. The stressfulness of their work was also evident in various biochemical measurements, and those workers who had most difficulty 'unwinding' experienced the most stress.

Sex differences and stress

Are women equally susceptible to such job-related stress? Do women respond to stress differently? Research indicates that indeed there are interesting and important sex differences, especially in this area of the ability to 'unwind'. Women manifest less biochemical reactivity than men in response to stressful and challenging situations and also tend to unwind more quickly.

But what happens when women take on traditional male roles or occupations? In one study, women students of engineering (in a class of which less than 5 per cent were women) displayed hormonal stress reactions more similar to those of men than to those of women following a more 'traditional' academic path. These findings raise interesting questions about whether women's new-found liberation will prove detrimental, at least in terms of a higher incidence of so-called male-related disorders such as coronary heart disease or ulcers. Similarly, one can ask if the changes in men's roles will reduce stress and raise their resistance to disease.

Some writers have speculated that such sex differences in response to stress may be associated with the greater vulnerability of men, as reflected in higher mortality rates. On average, women live about seven years longer than men. Does the way in which women cope with stress help to account for this difference? How important are different sex-roles in accounting for biochemical sex differences? As sex-roles change, will the differences between men and women in stress-related disorders and in mortality change? Future research will have to answer these important questions.

Personality factors in heart disease

The relationship between stress and illness is complicated. This is well illustrated in the research on coronary heart disease. Over one million people die each year in the United States from heart disease.

Could a stressful life style contribute to heart disease? Many clinicians have speculated about such a connection. As long ago as the late nineteenth century, clinicians repeatedly pointed to the hard-driving, goal-directed, aggressive qualities of coronary heart patients. In the 1930s and 1940s, the widespread occurrence of heart attacks stimulated a number of long-term studies to determine whether high-risk signs could be identified, thus making it possible to predict who might suffer a heart attack or other coronary heart disease. Of the various risk factors that have been identified, among them age, sex (being male), cigarette smoking, elevated systolic blood pressure, diabetes and family history of heart attacks, the one which most consistently predicted coronary heart disease was life style, or, in terms of this discussion, coping style.

In the 1950s, two cardiologists, Meyer Friedman and Ray Rosenman, were sufficiently impressed by their observations of post-coronary patients to begin a study of the role of personality factors in heart disease. On the basis of a relatively short 15-minute stress interview and a related questionnaire, they were able to classify individuals into two types, A and B, a small percentage of the population falling in between.

The type A label applies to individuals (mainly men) who are competitive and achievement-oriented, have a great sense of time-urgency and are prone to get angry. The converse of these traits characterizes the type B individuals. The psychologist Art Lewandowski neatly identified some A and B individuals. The subjects were asked to perform a letter-coding task under time-pressure and to list their thoughts immediately after the task.

The type A businessman said such things as 'I got self-critical—come on, you can go faster. You should be able to do it'; 'I've developed tests myself, so I got angry. What's this damn test for anyway?'; 'You're kidding. I can't believe it. I'm getting frustrated now. No'; 'Well, I'm an achiever, so I tried harder. I suspected the test may be a fake.'

This questionnaire is designed to assess Type A behaviour. It is based on the work of Friedman and Rosenman and was developed by Dr James Nora, Professor of Preventive Medicine at the University of Colorado School of Medicine.

Type A personality questionnaire

PLEASE TAKE YOUR TIME ANSWERING THESE QUESTIONS. It is important to give as frank an answer as possible. Feel free to ask your spouse or friends how you should answer the question. Some of these items, such as the way you talk, may not be apparent to you, but would be to those who know you well.

1 Do you feel there are not enough hours in the day to do all the things you must do?
( ) yes (✓) no

2 Do you always move, walk, and eat rapidly?
( ) yes (✓) no

3 Do you feel an impatience with the rate at which most events take place?
( ) yes (✓) no

4 Do you say, 'Uh-huh, uh-huh,' or 'yes, yes, yes, yes,' to someone who is talking, unconsciously urging him to 'get on with it' or hasten his rate of speaking? Do you have a tendency to finish the sentences of others for them?
( ) yes (✓) no

5 Do you become unduly irritated or even enraged when a car ahead of you in your lane runs at a pace you consider too slow? Do you find it anguishing to wait in line or to wait your turn to be seated in a restaurant?
(✓) yes ( ) no

6 Do you find it intolerable to watch others perform tasks you know you can do faster?
(✓) yes ( ) no

7 Do you become impatient with yourself as you are obliged to perform repetitive duties (making out bank deposit slips, writing cheques, washing and cleaning dishes, and so on), which are necessary but take you away from doing things you really have an interest in doing?

( ) yes (✓) no

8 Do you find yourself hurrying your own reading or always attempting to obtain condensations or summaries of truly interesting and worthwhile literature?

( ) yes (✓) no

9 Do you strive to think of or do two or more things simultaneously? For example, while trying to listen to another person's speech, do you persist in continuing to think about an irrelevant subject?

( ) yes (✓) no

10 While engaged in recreation, do you continue to ponder your business, home, or professional problems?

( ) yes (✓) no

11 Do you have (a) a habit of explosively accentuating various key words in your ordinary speech even when there is no real need for such accentuation, and (b) a tendency to utter the last few words of your sentences far more rapidly than the opening words?

( ) yes (✓) no

12 Do you find it difficult to refrain from talking about or bringing the theme of any conversation around to those subjects that especially interest and intrigue you, and when unable to accomplish this manoeuvre, do you pretend to listen but really remain preoccupied with your own thoughts?

( ) yes (✓) no

13 Do you almost always feel vaguely guilty when you relax and do absolutely nothing for several hours to several days?

( ) yes (✓) no

14 Do you attempt to schedule more and more in less and less time, and in doing so make fewer and fewer allowances for unforeseen contingencies?

( ) yes (✓) no

15 In conversation, do you frequently clench your fist or bang your hand upon a table or pound one fist into the palm of your hand in order to emphasize a conversational point?
(   ) yes   (✓) no

16 If employed, does your job include frequent deadlines that are difficult to meet?
(   ) yes   (✓) no

17 Do you frequently clench your jaw, or even grind your teeth?
(   ) yes   (✓) no

18 Do you frequently bring your work or study material (related to your job, not to school) home with you at night?
(   ) yes   (✓) no

19 Do you find yourself evaluating not only your own but also the activities of others in terms of numbers?
(✓) yes   (   ) no

20 Are you dissatisfied with your present work?
(✓) yes   (   ) no

Every *Yes* answer scores 1 point and every *No* answer 0. Total scores are broken down into the following categories: 4+ (14 or more points), 3+ (9−13 points), 2+ (4−8 points) and 1+ (3 or fewer points). Categories 2+ and 3+ are considered to be relatively neutral. A person who scores 4+ can consider himself significantly more at risk of a heart attack than 2+ or 3+ people; a 1+ person is least likely of all to have a heart attack.

In contrast, the type B businessman said 'I figured I'd go as well as I could anyway—besides, it's probably related to age and I'm not as young as I used to be'; 'I got uptight. Hey, you're getting keyed up—back off, relax. I tried to put my mind in limbo and did get better at the end'; 'I'm usually slow. I'm more interested in being right than breaking any speed records. I'm slower than average. Time is not my asset.'

Adjust or bust?

Throughout their performance, type A individuals became increasingly frustrated and annoyed with themselves, while the type B individuals adjusted their pace to the demands of the task. These general differences between type A and B individuals have been found by other investigators as well. They take on particular significance when we recall that type A individuals are more prone to have coronaries. Even when the variety of other risk factors is taken into account, type A men ran double the risk of developing coronary heart disease or dying than type B men. Among those patients who had had a heart attack, the risk of a subsequent attack among type A men was approximately twice that for type B men.

In considering these findings, it is necessary to repeat a warning made by the Canadian psychologist Ethel Roskies, an investigator of type A behaviour. The relationship between behavioural style and heart disease was studied mainly in a population of middle-aged, predominantly middle-class, white American males. Much research is currently underway on the relationship between type A behaviour and heart disease in blue-collar workers and in women. These comparisons are particularly important, since the manner in which type A behaviour may be manifested may vary according to the particular cultural group.

The urgent need for such research is indicated by the fact that Rosenman and Friedman estimated that about 10 per cent of urban employed men are type A, while one Canadian study reported that 76 per cent of a sample of managers were classified as type A. Roskies notes that, although individuals in professional and managerial occupations tend towards type A behaviour, this does not mean that type Bs cannot be found in management.

It is worth emphasizing that type A behaviour is more common among men than women in the USA, although differences between the sexes decline when women take on roles traditionally played by men. When differences in education and occupational level are considered, the women's type A scores do not differ from those of type A men. These results also suggest that changes in social roles may affect an individual's stress response, coping style and the resulting occurrence of disease.

As noted previously, one must ask what the potential costs of changing social roles are. Does the women's liberation movement mean that women, in their efforts to enter the job market and assume what were previously considered male roles, also increase the risk that they will contract stress-related illnesses? In turn, one may ask what will happen to men who change their roles. What are the consequences (perhaps positive) that go along with giving up the 'macho' aggressive achievement-oriented male role? Can society create social roles and jobs that do not exact such a heavy toll, for either men or women?

Type A behaviour is consistent with the transactional model of stress. The coronary-prone type A individual seems to behave in ways that add to the high risk of coronary disease. In this way, an individual's choice of life style contributes to the likelihood that he or she will encounter stress events. Just as one speaks of a coronary-prone life style, it may equally be possible to identify 'stress-prone' patterns of living. The conviction seems to be mounting that how people cope with stress may be even more important to overall morale, social functioning and health than the sheer frequency and severity of the stress episodes themselves.

The psychological impact of stress

When stress results from a sudden serious life event, such as a tornado, or a terrible accident to a relative, a more or less predictable pattern of response is evident. The affected person may react initially with an outcry, such as 'Oh no, no. It can't be true', or appear stunned and unable to take in the meaning of the loss. This is often followed by a phase of effective, well-controlled behaviour, especially in situations in which the person has to carry out specific routines (e.g., plan a funeral). Gradually, however, the multiple painful meanings of the event may lead to a variety of upsetting states of mind. The stressed individual may have flashback images, nightmares, pangs of emotion including rage, alienation, depersonalization or isolation from everyday life events, often accompanied by feelings of depression, guilt, shame, frustration and an impaired self-concept. Under undue stress, the individual's cognitive ability (problem-solving, memory, ability to focus attention) may be negatively affected as well. As time passes, most individuals cope adequately, but some do not.

Variable patterns of reaction

A number of false beliefs have been offered both by the lay public and by professionals to explain our reactions to stress. One such myth is that, following a life crisis, people go through a predictable, orderly set of reactions. In her popular book, *On Death and Dying*, Elizabeth Kubler-Ross suggests that individuals face up to death by going through a sequence of reactions—denial, anger, bargaining, depression and acceptance.

The results of more rigorous recent studies of stress indicate that life is not as orderly as Kubler-Ross and others have suggested, and have yielded findings inconsistent with a fixed sequence of emotional and coping reactions. There is little evidence for a set of predictable emotional reactions that follow in sequence. Indeed, much variety in the pattern of reactions is evident. Research on patients with spinal cord injuries as a result of an accident indicates that reactions such as anxiety and depression did not occur in a predictable sequence. These patients often experienced various emotional reactions simultaneously, or shifted back and forth between different reactions; for that matter, some skipped certain stages or did not reach others.

It is important to recognize this variability, so that we do not come to expect a certain stage of reaction and negatively view someone who has not experienced it, as often happens to people who have not shown depression or anger. There is no one formula, no 'right' or 'only' way to cope with stress.

Does 'time heal all'?

A related myth is that people will eventually accept or recover from stressful events. Elizabeth Kubler-Ross's model of how people cope with death implies that people will finally accept or come to terms with their impending demise. Elsewhere it is suggested that, because in time an individual will recover from an undesirable life event, one need not provide special help or do anything special. However, several studies have contradicted the belief that acceptance and recovery do occur. While many individuals do accept and recover from stressful life events, some do not.

In one study of women who had undergone mastectomy (removal of the breast because of cancer), some 30 per cent were reported to be severely upset (anxious and depressed) five years after the operation. Some 26 per cent of rape victims did not feel that they had recovered from their assault four to six years later. Studies of widows found that 25 per cent still felt sufficiently distressed at a two-year follow-up to seek psychiatric help. In yet another study, 40 per cent of the bereaved continued to experience intense anxiety two to four years after their loss. Studies of soldiers who suffered combat fatigue in the Second World War found that, 20 years later, some still suffered depression and restlessness. Vietnam combat veterans had a higher rate of mild to severe depression and anxiety one to five years after discharge than veterans who had not seen combat. If the combat veteran had lost a friend in battle, the likelihood of a depressive reaction increased.

For a sizeable minority, then, acceptance and recovery from serious stressful life events does not occur. True, many people find that emotional distress does gradually decline, and one puts one's life together again. But this is not always so. Some people may even experience what are called delayed stress reactions, in which unresolved conflicts and feelings surface years later. Among widows and widowers, one sometimes finds an 'anniversary reaction', namely a re-experiencing of the stress reaction—sadness, anxiety and so forth—on the date of the occurrence. Some people may experience such reactions conti-nuously for the rest of their lives.

4

The nature of coping

We have more ability than will-power, and it is
often an excuse to ourselves that we imagine
that things are impossible.

FRANÇOIS DE LA ROCHEFOUCAULD (1613–1680)

As we have seen, there are many situations in which a
sizeable minority of the population (e.g., rape victims,
victims of accidents, workers and others) fail to cope
with stress adequately and, in consequence, pay a
heavy price, both mentally and physically.

While there are many such instances of failure, at
the same time there are even more examples of how
people cope with profound losses, traumatic events
and daily hassles. Whether the stress is a result of
physical injury, disease, refugee status or the threat of
violence, individuals show remarkable adaptability
and courage. Research indicates that individuals
exposed to different types of stress—poverty, migra-
tion, psychotic parents, parental separation, divorce
and natural disasters—have resisted breakdown even
under dire circumstances. There are many healthy
people who have suffered extreme life crises and
many psychologically distressed people who have
experienced only a normal share of life's problems.

A tendency not to break down

When people are confronted with severe stress, they are much more resilient than might be expected. In an interesting book entitled *Fear and Courage*, the English psychologist S. J. Rachman has described people's response to air raids in the Second World War. Before the outbreak of the war, most authorities expected that air attacks on civilian targets would produce widespread panic, enduring terror and large numbers of psychiatric casualties. Accordingly, a number of psychiatric clinics were established to treat the future victims of the air raids. However, as Rachman wrote, 'to the considerable surprise of almost everyone, the psychological casualties were few, despite the death and destruction caused by the attacks'. Although there were some reports of depression, irritability and so forth, for the most part the raids produced only a slight increase in psychiatric disturbances, sometimes none at all.

Irving Janis, a psychologist who has studied people's reactions to extreme stress, also reported that the civilian population in Britain during the Second World War showed surprising equanimity. For example, fear reactions subsided within a quarter of an hour after the end of an air-raid. There was a rapid habituation to signals of danger (that is, reactions to repeated signs of danger became less intense). People paid little attention to the scream of the siren unless they could also hear the noise of bombs and aircraft. Fear of a bombing gave way to a 'business-as-usual' attitude.

The citizens of Hiroshima also showed an extraordinary resilience. The destruction, injuries, illness and death caused by this tragedy were of unprecedented magnitude and intensity. But, as Rachman states, 'given the scale of the trauma, the adverse effects were astonishingly, almost unbelievably, small in extent and intensity'. Within three months of the attack some 140 000 people had returned to the city.

It's worth looking, too, at the findings of the Israeli sociologist Aaron Antonovsky. He claims that over 25 per cent of those who survived internment in a concentration camp did so without succumbing to psychiatric disorders or chronic physical disease, despite their long years of physical suffering under the constant threat of death, amid terrible atrocities.

Such resilience and courage are not only demonstrated under the intense stress of war. Investigations of reactions to disasters have reported a general lifting of morale in the stricken population. For example, after the San Francisco earthquake and fire in 1906, the famous psychologist William James was impressed by 'the speed with which people improvised order out of chaos and by the universal equanimity of the survivors and by the cheerfulness and helpfulness they exhibited'.

People's ability to respond with remarkable speed, common sense and basic humanity to urgent needs following major catastrophes such as earthquakes, floods and tornadoes has been repeatedly reported. There are also many accounts of people's ability to cope with the stress of various diseases, including asthma, diabetes, cystic fibrosis, hearing disabilities, blindness, burns, cancer, colostomies, haemophilia and scoliosis.

A quote from a report by Visotsky and his colleagues, who studied how patients coped with acute poliomyelitis, shows that people can satisfactorily adapt to their predicament.

> 'Many patients are remarkably resourceful even in the face of a catastrophic situation. Though our patients were deprived for long periods—and sometimes permanently—of abilities which are part of basic human equipment, most of them nevertheless showed an impressive resilience and the ability to work out new patterns of living.'

What is coping?

The term 'coping' refers to the responses made by an individual who encounters a situation with a poten-

tially harmful outcome. We use an enormous repertoire of response strategies to cope with diverse
demands. We may use these coping strategies in
many different combinations and at different times.
Strategies successful and appropriate in one situation
may not be especially appropriate on another occasion; nor will the strategies appropriate at one time
necessarily be effective later.

Some effort has been made to categorize these
diverse coping reactions and, in general, two major
functions of coping have been identified. One function of coping is to alter the situation that is causing the
stress: problem-oriented coping consists of efforts to
deal with the source of the stress by changing the
environment either by direct actions or by changing
one's behaviour. The second function of coping is
emotion regulation: coping efforts aimed at reducing
emotional distress. These two modes of coping may be
used in different combinations.

Changing the situation

For example, consider the stress caused by urban
noise and the direct action that can be taken to avoid or
reduce it. One study measured the effects of aircraft
noise on children at an elementary school below the
air corridor leading to Los Angeles International
Airport. Children in 'high-noise' schools (one flight
every 2·5 minutes) had higher blood pressure, were
more likely to fail and not persist on problem-solving
tasks and had lower maths and reading scores than
children in 'quieter' schools. The children in the
noisier schools were also more easily distracted.
Children living on the higher, and therefore quieter,
floors of apartment buildings subject to heavy traffic
noise have been found to do better at school than
those living on the lower floors. In these circumstances, one might take direct action to avoid or
reduce the stress of urban noise through urban
planning, social protest and other legal and political
methods. In certain situations, we can avoid and
reduce stress by trying directly to alter the physical
and social environment.

Reducing emotional distress

In other situations in which we cannot alter or avoid the situation, we may use what are called 'palliative' ways of coping—ways of responding that make us feel better in the face of threat and harm without resolving the problem. In such situations, we may use various techniques to regulate our emotional distress. Sometimes we may decide not to think about it, at other

times we may remain detached, adopting a philo-sophical stance in order to rationalize aspects of the situation (e.g., 'it can't be all that bad'), even deceiving ourselves as to the seriousness of the problem. Some people use relaxation or meditation as a palliative remedy: far more common is the use of alcohol or tranquillizers.

When such palliative techniques are used excess-ively, the coping response itself (denial, alcohol and so on) may become the problem. All too often, prescrip-tion drugs are used as a major coping response. One researcher, Judy Mundey, has provided a fine ex-ample of how drugs have become the prescribed way to cope with stress.

> 'A friend once told me she felt she was living in a volcano. She worked full-time as a shop assistant, was married, had two children in primary school and cared for her aged father who also lived with them. Her husband, a low earner with subsequent financial problems, tried to forget (or drown) them by frequent heavy drinking. He took out the resultant remorse on his wife . . . A doctor prescribed Valium (a mild tranquillizer) for her headaches.'

Drugs to the rescue

The cost of drugs used to combat stress runs into hundreds of millions of dollars. It has been estimated that, in Great Britain, one woman in five and one man in ten takes mind-altering prescription drugs, and

one man in ten takes mind-altering drugs...

about one million Britons are on Valium; in the USA, some 15 per cent are on anti-stress drugs. These numbers are increasing. Over the past 20 years, taking tranquillizers has become the socially acceptable way to cope when beset by anxiety and stress.

These figures are particularly significant for women, who are the major consumers of prescribed psychotropic drugs (tranquillizers, stimulants, anti-depressants). At least half the adult women in the USA have used psychotropic drugs at some time. In 1977, of 51 million Americans who used tranquillizers, 63 per cent were women. Of 17 million individuals who used medically prescribed stimulants, 71 per cent were women. Women also received 71 per cent of the prescriptions for antidepressants. Each year in the USA, 8 500 000 women are prescribed tranquillizers for the first time, 3 000 000 sedatives and 1 000 000 stimulants.

In Western societies, one major way to cope with stress-related problems has been to prescribe medication, especially for women. It should be noted that taking a drug such as Valium is not a benign way of coping. Recent research indicates that one side-effect of such a drug is the difficulty of withdrawal. Barbara Gordon's book *I Am Dancing as Fast as I Can* (1980) describes one woman's struggle to free herself from such drug dependence.

Active and passive responses

The emotion-regulation method thus demonstrates that successful coping does not always involve active mastery over one's environment. Retreat, toleration or disengagement may be the most healthy response in certain circumstances.

In many non-Western cultures, people adopt a fatalism that can serve a positive function. For example, in the Philippines the phrase *Bahala na!* (which, loosely translated, means 'it's up to God' or 'it's not in my hands') often serves a useful function in coping with stress. Such expressions reflect the belief held in some cultures that it is better to accept events than to persist in trying to change that which may be unchangeable. In many cultures—the Mexican, for instance—people tend to deal with the stresses of life passively by trying to endure them. This is in sharp contrast with Americans, who usually actively attempt to modify the environment in some fashion.

In summary, we may try to change the situation for the better if we can, or we may try to manage our stress-related emotions so they do not get out of hand. People often use a mixture of both direct action and palliative forms of coping. Instead of becoming over-dependent upon any one coping response (drugs or whatever), a more moderate coping strategy should be followed. The serenity prayer of Alcoholics Anonymous is a magnificent expression of the moderation strategy: 'God grant me the serenity to accept things I cannot change, courage to change the things I can, and the wisdom to know the difference.'

The complexity of the coping response

We can see another example of the complexity of the coping process in a comprehensive study by Leonard Pearlin and Carmi Schooler. They interviewed 2 300 adults aged between 18 and 65, living in Chicago, about the causes of stress in their lives (conflicts, frustrations, and so on) and how they tried to cope with them. Three types of coping were distinguished. First, some coping responses tried to change the situation and solve the problem. These included direct actions such as talking things out with someone, trying to find a compromise, talking to others to find a solution, or taking action to get rid of the difficulties (e.g., altering what they were asked to do at work).

A second type of coping took the form of controlling the meaning of the stressful situation after it occurred, but before the stress emerged. One can control the meaning of a situation by ignoring certain reactions of other people or positively comparing oneself with them. Thoughts such as 'count your blessings' and 'we're all in the same boat' are all attempts to control the meaning of a situation.

The third effort to cope was designed to control the stress itself after it had emerged. Passive acceptance and withdrawal and thoughts such as 'take the bad with the good', 'try not to worry because time itself solves problems' and 'everything works out for the best' are examples of this style of coping.

Pearlin and Schooler reported that the keynote to good coping was the ability to be flexible in shifting from one coping response to another as the situation demanded. It is important to have a variety of weapons (coping skills) in one's arsenal. A flexible repertoire is the best resistance to stress.

Good coping and poor coping

The Pearlin and Schooler study also indicated that no one can be characterized as being resistant to stress. We can, however, characterize 'good' and 'poor' copers. If people are described as 'good copers', it generally means that they maintain an 'even keel' most of the time when confronted with life events widely recognized as stressful. In contrast, the 'poor coper' is frequently thrown off balance by events that are not normally regarded as threatening.

Major or minor periods of coping breakdown or failure to adapt may be observed in both the 'good coper' and the 'poor coper'. Each of us has a breaking-point; each of us is vulnerable under the right conditions. What appears to distinguish the 'good' from the 'poor' coper is the frequency, intensity or duration of the coping breakdown, as well as the time needed to recover. The ability to rebound from stressful events is an important feature in the coping process.

Often it is difficult to determine exactly what good coping is. What may appear to be good coping in the

short run (not over-reacting, for instance) may not always prove beneficial in the long run. Defining 'good' coping becomes even more difficult when we learn that some types of coping may relate best to certain indices of adjustment or outcome measures, such as vocational adjustment, while other types are better predictors of other indices such as marital satisfaction. When we ask, 'Is this a "good" coping response?', we may also have to ask, 'What type of outcome do you have in mind?'

Another example of the complexity of the coping response is illustrated in a study of people learning to become parachutists. The investigators (Ursin and his colleagues) found that, with practice, parachutists develop a basic trust in their skills and in their ability to

I'd cope better if the chute opened...

handle the situation. Most interestingly, this sense of self-confidence was evident in the jumpers' verbal judgement as indicated on a questionnaire and in a decrease in the biochemical hormonal levels that signify stress. These changes were evident long before experts had rated the parachutists' performance as improved.

Defining which responses 'work'

The research on the parachutists provides a much-needed warning. We should be cautious in evaluating the effectiveness of any particular coping response. Whether it works or not will be influenced by factors such as: when it is used; its appropriateness for the situation; how far the individual is confident of the technique; the degree to which other coping responses are available; and the index of coping used to assess its efficacy. Some coping responses (such as denial) may 'work' to the extent of a person saying that he or she feels calm; yet, at the physical level, stress disturbance may still be powerfully at work.

In short, the evaluation of any particular coping response is complex and we should be cautious in prescribing or endorsing specific coping procedures. For some individuals, for some problems, for some situations, · denial may be most useful. On other occasions, the same person may find problem-solving or humour the most useful response. In fact, the same person may use different coping responses at different times to handle the same stressor. Once again, the need for flexibility and caution is clearly indicated.

Shifting between coping strategies

To show the complexity of the coping process, I should like to cite a study carried out at the Massachusetts General Hospital. Researchers here (Weisman, Worden, Sobel) studied how cancer patients cope with their illness and its treatment. They found that there are significant differences between those who cope well and those who experience greater emotional distress. These differences cannot be

TWO REACTIONS TO STRESS...

accounted for solely in terms of the patient's physical state: some patients with advanced cancer cope better than others who later showed no evidence of the disease.

The most effective copers confronted their problems directly and tended to look upon their situation as a problem to be solved. Although they were rather independent and self-reliant, they did not hesitate to use other resources when necessary. If they felt neglected, they insisted on more information and better treatment. They resourcefully shifted from one coping strategy to another. Good coping consisted of (a) optimism, an expectation that positive change is possible; (b) practicality about the kinds of solutions feasible; (c) flexibility in not insisting upon a rigid approach to any problem; and (d) resourcefulness in finding support or additional information that might help to implement coping strategies.

Two stories of survival

This adaptive coping style is shown particularly clearly in the case of one cancer patient, a 67-year-old widow, one of whose breasts was removed about six months after her husband's death. She had already been in hospital more than 20 times for a variety of ailments. Despite serious physical disability, she had managed to care for an ailing husband for ten years, as well as for two abandoned grandchildren, one of whom had lung disease. To complicate matters further, both her supportive sister and brother-in-law had recently died, leaving her quite alone. Even though there were inadequate funds, she managed to keep a job and did not seek public assistance. What is remarkable is that this woman experienced very low emotional distress. She voiced no resentment about her plight and seemed to take satisfaction from whatever she was called upon to do. Her 'take things as they come' attitude, her style of viewing each challenge as a problem to be solved, as a task to work at assiduously and not to worry over, her ability to divide major events into tasks to be handled step-by-step all helped her to cope with the stress of her life.

While some patients such as this widow naturally acquire and employ effective coping skills, other less competent copers require counselling. In Chapter 7 we will consider the type of counselling offered to help stressed patients to cope more effectively.

My second example is taken from research into Holocaust victims. A number of interviews were conducted with survivors of the Nazi concentration camps to determine how they were able to survive and cope with stress. One investigator, Joel Dimsdale, reported on the variety of different coping styles used to survive unbelievable brutalization and degradation. These included the following:

1 Differential focus on the good: many inmates focused their attention on small gratifications, such as getting through the food line without a beating, and thus attempted to ignore the larger tragedies of the camps.

2 Survival for some purpose: others felt a need to survive to help a relative, to bear witness and show the world what had happened, or to seek revenge.

3 Psychological removal: this strategy involved insulating oneself from stress by developing ways of not feeling any emotion. One individual had developed a delusion that the soldiers raping and abusing her were devils incarnate and that she was above their assaults.

4 Concept of mastery: this consisted of an attempt to find one area in which the individual did not feel defeated by stress. Humour also played an important role in the survival process.

5 Group affiliation: such affiliation gave important support by providing information, advice, protection and a source of identification.

Humour as a coping response

Humour is another way of coping with both daily and extreme stress. Take, for example, the story of the man who is about to be shot by a firing squad: when asked if he would like a last cigarette, he refuses, saying, 'No thanks, I'm trying to give them up.' Such humour is an attempt to cope with the stress and fear of death. Both laughter and tears seem to release stress.

Recently Norman Cousins, a well-known American magazine editor, wrote a moving account of his own serious physical illness and how he used 'positive emotions' produced by comic movies and humorous television programmes to help him recover. If stress and negative emotions can contribute to disease, perhaps positive emotions, especially humour and laughter, may have a healing and preventive impact.

In conclusion, we should remember that the coping process is not a single act, nor is it static. Coping is a constellation of many acts that stretch over time and undergo change. At the moment, it is impossible to determine which types of coping work best for particular people in certain circumstances. Several factors that influence the coping process have been determined, however, and it is to these that we now turn.

5

What influences the coping process?

– When a man prays, do you know what he's doing? – He's saying to himself: 'Keep calm, everything's all right; it's all right.'

UGO BETTI (1892–1953)

If one analyses the coping process, three psychological factors—a sense of personal control, adequate information and social support—can be seen to play a particularly important role.

Feeling in control

The statement: 'If I could stop the roller-coaster, I wouldn't want to get off' sums up this topic. A number of laboratory studies have shown that, when people believe they can exercise some influence over the occurrence or termination of unpleasant events such as loud noises or electric shocks, their physiological arousal is reduced and their performance improves. In contrast, those who do not believe they have personal control show substantially greater stress reactions. Mere belief in one's sense of control reduces the level of stress.

The opportunity to exercise control

In a typical study, a group of people were exposed to tape-recordings of loud, randomly occurring noise, including people speaking foreign languages and office equipment in operation. The effect was a jumbled roar, rather like much day-to-day urban noise. While exposed to this noise, subjects were asked to do a number of tasks requiring persistence and attention to detail (e.g., puzzles and proof-reading). Half the people taking part in the experiment were provided with a button that enabled them to terminate the noise; they were told to use the button only if the noise became too much to bear. The other

If this PLANE lands safely I promise NEVER to complain again about feeling stressful...

half had no button. As the researchers had predicted, subjects with access to the 'off switch' attempted almost five times as many insoluble puzzles and made significantly fewer mistakes in proof-reading than their button-less counterparts.

The importance of these results lies in the fact that those who had potential control did *not* exercise it. No one used the button to stop the noise; knowing it was there proved to be enough to change the character of the situation. The realization that something could be done about the noise reduced the effects of stress.

There are many counterparts to this laboratory exercise in real life. Consider a study conducted in Sweden in the winter of 1973–4, when petrol rationing was imposed. Rationing meant that the trains were crowded. The stress level of commuters before and during the rationing period was assessed, and, as expected, their stress did increase. Although seats were available for all passengers at all times, the stress response was lowest among those who were able to select a seat and choose their own company. Passengers who boarded the train at its first stop experienced less stress than those who boarded midway when the train was already crowded and seat selection was restricted. Some passengers even drove to the first station so that they had the freedom to choose, thus reducing their stress. Exerting control by means of direct action enabled them to decrease their stressful reactions.

Faith and fear

People also attempt to cope with stress through religion and prayer. The saying 'you don't find atheists in foxholes' confirms the results of several surveys of soldiers. In one study of combat soldiers in the Second World War, three-quarters of the infantrymen questioned said that prayer helped a great deal to control intense fear, while 60 per cent of the airmen surveyed in another study reported that prayer helped them to cope with stress. An individual's belief system or world view (in this case religion) provides a sense of coherence and a means of coping with stress. For some, this sense of coherence makes frustration, failure and pain more tolerable.

Free will versus destiny

We all differ in the degree of personal control we experience. Some people generally hold what has been called an 'internal' view of control, whereby they feel that generally they can exert control over the environment. They believe that they are masters of their own fate. In contrast, people with an 'external' focus of control feel that generally they are the victims of circumstance and fate. Events, they believe, are normally beyond their influence.

Research suggests that our attitude to personal control influences how much stress we experience and how we cope. People who do not view themselves as effective copers are more likely to see stressful events as personally threatening. People with more confidence are more likely either to evaluate situations as challenging, or not to view the situation as threatening or challenging and merely dismiss it. Those who have a greater sense of control are more likely to initiate change, engage in direct actions, seek information or mobilize others than those with a lower sense of personal control.

The fact that political and social activists tend to be better educated, possess greater self-pride and a stronger ability to influence events in their lives, and feel a greater sense of personal control, illustrates these differences and contradicts the belief that 'hopelessness breeds militant action'. Instead, it appears that individuals who lead tend to have a sense of control that helps them to cope with stress.

In contrast, those who feel that they lack control often develop what is called a sense of 'learned helplessness'. This term describes a person's belief that his actions have no influence on the outcome of events, that nothing he does makes any difference. If one cannot—or, at least, if one has the impression that one cannot—offset stressful situations by one's own

actions, then feelings of helplessness and hopelessness develop. These reactions may spread and may
eventually lead to anxiety and depression.

Information as ammunition

Another factor influencing the coping process is the
nature, amount and timing of the information
available. As the saying goes, 'forewarned is fore-
armed'. Information is like a road map that tells
individuals what they are likely to experience.

In general, the more information we have about the
nature of a stressful event—when it is likely to happen
and how long it will last, and its preliminary signs
—the more likely we are to find ways of preventing
it occurring or reducing its consequences.

The accuracy of someone's expectations of an
impending event is critical in determining his emotional state. The more accurate the expectation, the
less likely he is to become emotional and stressful. For
example, astronauts are trained to have contingency
plans and problem-solving strategies available to meet
all imaginable emergencies. In this way, an emer-
gency will more than likely become another routine
situation. Stress is most likely to occur when no action
or thought structures are available to handle the
situation.

Knowing what to expect

Most of the research suggesting the potential value of
information has come from work with hospital
patients about to undergo surgery or a difficult
medical examination. For example, a set of studies by
Jean Johnson and Howard Leventhal examined the
role of preparatory communication in helping patients
to prepare for a medical endoscopic examination (a
diagnostic examination used to study the stomach,
intestines and other organs, in which a tube has to be

lowered through the mouth into the organ in question). The night before, patients were given information about the sensory experiences they would encounter (e.g., they would feel the prick of the needle given to make them drowsy; they would gag when their throat was swabbed to anaesthetize it; their stomach would feel full when they were pumped with air) and coping information (e.g., breathe through the mouth while the throat is being swabbed; make swallowing motions when swallowing the tube).

On a variety of coping measures (gagging during the examination, time taken to swallow the tube, signs of fear and co-operation, amount of drugs given to make the patient drowsy, heart rate) patients given preparatory information showed less stress than those without it. Being informed about what to expect helped to reduce the stress response. Such preparatory information gives people the opportunity to 'prelive' the experience or to conduct a mental rehearsal, what has come to be called the 'work of worrying'.

Two sorts of worrying

The constructive 'work of worrying' and 'neurotic worrying' must be distinguished. A neurotic worrier is unlikely to attain emotional mastery of the threat, but instead replays in his mind's eye a number of catastrophes, usually with accompanying self-deprecating thoughts and feelings. The 'work of worrying', by contrast, involves a form of anticipatory preparation, in which the individual rehearses how to deal with realistic threats. Such constructive thoughts serve to ward off anticipated trauma and to overcome the painful effects of past traumas.

It is important to understand that not all patients respond to preparatory information in a uniform fashion. Some patients, who have been described as 'repressors', may be better off with distraction procedures than with preparatory communication. Characteristically, these 'repressors' cope with stress by not thinking about it, by denying it, or simply by not recognizing any potential stress. In contrast, 'sensitizers'—those who characteristically cope with stress by seeking information about a stressor or engaging in the 'work of worrying'—benefit from preparatory communication.

Thus, when setting up an information programme to help individuals to cope with the stress of events such as surgery, it is necessary to be sensitive to differences between individuals and not to treat everyone in the same way.

Discussion of 'repressors' raises an important topic, namely the use of denial as a coping response. In some instances, people may avoid preparatory information, distort it or simply deny it. For example, the study of flood victims discussed on page 22 reported that some people denied that a flood could recur, believing that the previous flood had been a freak, or placing great emphasis on new forms of flood control.

The question to be asked is when does such denial help to reduce stress and when is it maladaptive, thus engendering stress?

'It's not happening'

Denial is usually viewed as a maladaptive or ineffective coping response, because the stark reality of the stressful situation has to be faced at some point.

Few events can be considered as stressful as the fatal illness of a child. The reaction is helpless, desperate, yet unbelieving. 'No, not my child. There must be some answer. There must be some hope. I won't accept it. I can't accept it.' It is likely that some people will deceive themselves in order to maintain hope. At one level, one can accept the reality of the situation, of what the doctors say, but at another level an inner anger, a sense of injustice cries out and may prevent acceptance. Under these conditions, denial may serve a useful coping purpose. The individual is self-protective, and denial may facilitate gradual exposure to the stressor. Denial may be a way of learning to pace oneself, handling only so much stress at one time and slowly increasing exposure as one gradually assimilates the meaning of the information.

When denial is appropriate and constructive

But under what conditions can denial be an adaptive, coping response? Consider a situation in which the stress is likely to abate with little effort on the individual's part. In such cases direct action is irrelevant, for failure to deal with the problem does not affect its outcome; the individual may have nothing to lose from not attending to the stress. In situations in which little or nothing can be done—when, for instance, there is constant fear of terrorist attacks or war or the uncertainty of political and social upheaval—there may be value in using denial in order to feel better and maintain hope and a sense of self-worth.

Denial also includes what is called intellectualization—thoughts such as 'There's no danger, it won't affect me', or 'The chances it'll affect me are 1 000 to 1'—or maintaining detachment ('It's not my problem'), or even self-deception ('Don't worry, I can handle anything').

Denial may be especially appropriate when there is a built-in likelihood of a fortuitous outcome, where, for example, not attending to or not trying to solve the problem associated with the stress may be the best solution. When in your own life would it be best not to expend energy needlessly or worry unproductively? Are there some occasions when not doing anything or not thinking about a problem would be the best solution, when absence of action and the use of denial might prevent further stress? On the other hand, if the stress is likely to be permanent or lethal if left unattended, then a coping style that consists of avoidance may prevent the individual taking appropriate steps.

Denial may serve two purposes. First, it dampens ideas and feelings that might distract the individual from action needed immediately. In some senses, denial (or not thinking about some events) acts as a filter that concentrates attention on those tasks that warrant immediate concern. Second, denial allows an individual to adjust gradually to unpleasant information and events or to 'dose' himself or herself strategically with needed information. For example, weakened and helpless victims of severe illnesses (such as polio, burns and spinal cord injuries) often use denial at first in order to cope with the stress of this most debilitating early stage. Later, as they begin rehabilitation, they shift to a more direct means of coping. The constructive value of denial is that it helps individuals not to become overwhelmed and provides the time needed to marshal other coping resources.

When denial is destructive

There are, however, occasions when denial can retard coping, as, for instance, when women deny the significance of lumps in their breasts or men experience a heart attack but deny the significance of the pain. For women in such situations, denial can take several forms, from avoidance of self-examination to denial of the potential significance of the lumps. Some men, even while suffering from a heart attack, may try to deny its existence by taking vigorous exercise. Here, obviously, the medical dangers are too great for denial to serve any useful purpose as a coping strategy.

A case study of a middle-aged man who failed for over a year to respond to increasingly severe symptoms of lung disease provides another example of the potential dangers of denial. He finally agreed to surgery after considerable family pressure. His responses in the pre-operation interview gave compelling evidence of his use of denial. His case notes tell us:

'He doubted that his illness was serious, asserting that he could probably get along quite well without the operation but that, since everyone said he should have it, he was willing to give it a try. During the interview, the patient made many joking, facetious remarks, and behaved in such a way as to give the interviewer an impression of forced gaiety. When asked the standard series of questions about his expectations and feelings concerning the impending operation, he responded in a stereotyped manner, mechanically shrugged his shoulders, grinned, and remarked: "What's the use of worrying? I've got nothing to worry about." ' (Janis, 1958)

This patient died of advanced lung cancer 11 months after the surgery. In a very real sense, his denial cost him his life.

Other aspects of denial

Finally, an intriguing set of studies of novice and experienced parachutists highlight the complex function of denial. Beginner parachutists used an all-or-none type of control, either completely avoiding thinking about the stress related to the jump or else feeling overwhelmed at times. Some of the novice parachutists appeared remarkably unconcerned well before a jump, but often had an attack of anxiety when it was imminent. When this happened, some even gave up jumping. One experienced jump-master stated:

> 'If I am taking a student up, I like to see him a little uneasy; it is natural that he should be. I had one particular chap one day, he was too relaxed . . . he jumped into the airplane, and when he got up there, he said "No, I am not going." Now, I knew before he even got up there that he was not going to jump . . . if this fellow does jump, and he hasn't got this, well, uneasiness, you know, he makes a jump and might kill himself.' (Fenz, 1975).

This rigid, all-or-none type of defence means that the denial of anxiety is a poor form of adaptation, as it cannot be maintained when the individual must actively face the threat. Consequently, as the parachutists developed mastery and self-confidence, the psychological defences they used to handle the stress of parachuting changed. In such highly threatening situations, denial can help to protect an individual from being overwhelmed.

Social support

At the moment, there is a great deal of interest in how the social environment or community (family, friends, neighbours) can be used to help people to cope with stress. The term 'social support' refers to personal contacts available to an individual from other individuals, groups and the community. Individuals may belong to several such groups—at home, at work, at church, in their leisure pursuits, and so on.

Social supports provide the individual with a means of expressing his or her feelings, finding meaning in crises with others, receiving material aid, providing information, developing realistic goals and receiving feedback. In general, people with established support networks (e.g., close relationships with family members, friends, co-workers) are in better mental physical health and cope better with stress than unsupported individuals. People who live alone and who are not involved with other people or with organizations are more vulnerable to a variety of chronic diseases.

There are some interesting studies that show how a support group helps people to cope with stress. In one case, eight crewmen from the wreck of a small cargo vessel drifted for nine days on a raft in rough seas, one man dying. Interviews with the seven survivors showed that one very important way of coping was thinking about loved ones:

> 'Everyone thought how would we survive in this—we were thinking about our families. I just kept thinking about my wife and family—that was all I had to live for. We all talked about our families. I told them about my missus . . . It does pass through your mind "Will she be alright?" [Of his children] I thought of them a lot. Even when I paddled, I used to recite their names . . . I'd go right through them. I think it helped. It gave me determination. (He then indicated how he said a child's name with each paddle stroke.)' (Henderson and Bostock, 1975)

The survivors depended upon their support system (their fellow-survivors and their closest family members) to help them cope with a life-threatening experience. Interestingly, a two-year follow-up assessment of the survivors found that only two men were living satisfying lives, even feeling that their ordeal had somehow strengthened them. The others had sought help for a variety of psychological complaints including anxiety, depression, insomnia and nightmares.

A problem shared . . .

On the whole, we manifest less fear and stress and greater courage in the presence of others than alone. Somehow, the presence of others acts as a buffer to stress responses. The value of the social group in facilitating the coping process has been highlighted by studies of combat soldiers and airmen, among whom the social group is a primary motivating force in coping with stress. One of the most important incentives for the soldiers was the need to support and assist their comrades, the feeling that one should not 'let one's buddies down'. If too many soldiers within a given combat unit (approximately 65 per cent) are wounded or killed, then the number of stress-related disorders (e.g., combat exhaustion) in the remaining soldiers increases substantially.

In many cases it is not the number of social contacts, but rather the quality of the relationships that influences the coping process. In one study, it was found that women who shared an intimate relationship with a friend, lover or husband were 90 per cent less likely to become depressed than women who had no such relationship to turn to. Similarly, men who had all the symptoms associated with the development of painful heart seizures were much less likely to develop such seizures if they had a warm relationship with their wives. Workers made redundant were less likely to become depressed and ill if they had a supportive marital relationship.

While more research is needed to explain exactly how support systems help people to cope with stress, it is important to appreciate that such support systems can play an important role in the coping process.

The threefold approach to coping

An interesting example of how personal control, information and social support can be combined to cope with stress is shown by David Mechanic, a sociologist. He has studied how university students prepared for taking nine two-hour qualifying exams and, in particular, how they coped with stress as the examinations approached. Mechanic describes how the students sought social support from other students, friends, wives, faculty and, sometimes, anyone who was present. They also used comforting thoughts to help them to control their emotional reactions, among them:

'I'm as bright and knowledgeable as other students who have passed these examinations.'

'I've handled test situations in the past—there's no good reason why not now.'

'I am doing all I can to prepare—the rest is not up to me.'

'I wouldn't have gotten this far unless I knew something.'

'I'm well liked in this department. I've already demonstrated my competence on past work, they will pass me. You can't fail these examinations unless you really mess up.'

In addition to these thoughts, the students used humour and positive social comparisons with other students to cope with their stress. These techniques were employed on top of some very hard studying. The variety of different responses used was part of the coping process.

6

A self-help approach

The bow too tensely strung is easily broken.

PUBLIUS SYRUS (1st century BC)

So far, we have found out that the coping process is complex, and that stress has many causes and many effects. There is no single or simple formula for managing stress. In some instances, an adequate coping response may be to change the situation for the better if we can; in other situations, we may use techniques that make us feel better in the face of threat or harm.

The keynote is flexibility. It is more effective to possess a variety of coping skills than one specific response. The ability to tailor a particular coping response to the demands of the situation is critical; there is no prescribed sequence of coping responses. Coping techniques must be sensitive to both individual and cultural differences. Each of us prefers to cope in particular ways, and these ways are in part influenced by our own particular cultural group. One should be cautious about so-called fixed 'packages' of coping techniques.

We know, too, that the way we think about events, how we perceive stress and our ability to handle it, influence its impact on us. Our attitudes towards stressful events, our prior experience of them, our knowledge of their possible effects, our evaluation of the costs and benefits involved—all these influence our stress reaction. When a stress is familiar, when it occurs at a definite time and place, and when we sense that we can handle it, then our reactions will be less intense. If we can prepare for the stress by mental rehearsal or by 'constructive worrying', the stress will prove more manageable. Preparatory information can often help you to start thinking creatively about the problem.

We should also remember that graded exposure to less threatening stressful events has a beneficial effect. There is a need to pace the mastery of stress in order to cope with limited amounts of stress at a time. Gradual exposure to small amounts of stress before entering a high-pressure situation can boost an individual's defence against stress. In this way a sense of self-confidence can be established. Just as we do not try to learn a new skill such as skiing by beginning on the steepest hill, we should try to learn to cope with stress in similar fashion, pacing ourselves. Finally, we can use the help of others to avoid and reduce stress.

These general guidelines can be translated into a step-by-step approach which will improve the ability to cope with stress.

Step one: know yourself

The first step in any programme that sets out to change behaviour—be it smoking, overeating or stressful reactions—is to increase the individual's awareness of his or her present behaviour, and of the events that precede, accompany and follow the reaction or behaviour. One must break the automatic reflexive manner in which we behave and learn to interrupt this behavioural chain.

For example, some chain-smokers do not even realize that they have started another cigarette; nor can they tell you how many cigarettes they have smoked until they count the butts in the ashtray. Similarly, in the case of stress we must become aware of low-intensity cues, the first signs of the stress reaction, so that eventually we can interrupt the pattern, or chain of events, with more adaptive coping responses. It is easier to interrupt the cycle of behaviour when it is at a low intensity, when the stress reaction is just beginning, than when it is full-blown, filled with emotion.

Mental rehearsal

One way to become aware of these signs is to close your eyes and imagine a scene when you are stressed. Play in your mind's eye, in slow motion, what happened before, during and after the stressful event. What thoughts and images preceded, accompanied and followed the situation? A parent imagining putting four children to bed can in this way become aware of how his thoughts and feelings contributed to the problem and engendered stress.

Which stressful scenes do you conjure up? Are your thoughts and feelings similar in each stressful situation? Do certain agenda, current concerns, thoughts and feelings always occur? Do certain themes emerge, such as a sense of injustice, a concern with independence, a desire to achieve? Current concerns of this kind may play an important role in determining what you find stressful.

In what situations do you feel stressed?

Make a list of the situations in which you feel stressed, and rate each of these on a three-point scale from very stressful (3), to moderately stressful (2), to mildly stressful (1). How do the situations rated 3 differ from those rated 1? What are the common elements among the situations rated 3? How did you know you were stressed in each situation? What bodily signs indicated that you were stressed? Could you tell that you were stressed from the reactions of those around you? In some ways you can become your own Sherlock Holmes, trying to identify and understand those clues that signal stress.

In short, the first step towards improving your ability to cope with stress is to 'know thyself' and the kinds of impact you have on others. Stress is transactional—we are not mere victims of it. To prove this, it may be useful to monitor your own reactions by keeping a daily diary of the stressors you encounter and of the way your own reactions may have contributed to the degree of stress experienced. Never forget that, no matter how stressful you feel, there is someone else who has felt just as stressed in a similar situation; but somehow they managed, coped. How did they cope? What can you do to improve your ability to cope with stress?

Coping with stress involves more than understanding. It also involves ensuring that your self-analysis leads to a variety of specific things you can do. We will now discuss briefly various major coping responses.

Relax

One of the most popular pieces of advice runs, 'Just relax. Keep cool. Take it easy.' This is often easier said than done. In fact, many people complain that they don't know how to relax. The word 'workaholics' describes them well—people who are so preoccupied with work that even their vacations are stressful.

In 1938, the physician Edmund Jacobson developed a progressive relaxation-training procedure, lasting 50 to 200 sessions, in which specific muscle groups were intensively tensed and released. Since Jacobson's pioneer work, a good deal about progressive relaxation has been learned. First, such relaxation exercises can be done in significantly fewer sessions; as few as four to eight may be sufficient. Second, relaxation is a skill, and like any other skill it requires practice. Several audio-tapes of relaxation exercises are now available, and people can practise at home. As the skill develops, relaxation, especially slow, deep breathing, can be used as an active coping skill that controls physical tension and stress. Third, mental relaxation is a key part of the physical relaxation process. Some of us relax by engaging in strenuous exercise (swimming, walking, jogging), others by becoming absorbed in a task (gardening, knitting), still others by meditating or engaging in progressive relaxation by tensing and releasing the various muscle groups of the body.

How does relaxation help?

Whatever form relaxation takes, there is evidence to suggest that it does reduce physiological arousal, tenseness and the level of stress. For example, a survey showed that people who felt overwhelmed by their jobs tried to keep calm by saying some of the following things to themselves:

'Try to tread water for a few days and catch your breath. Calm yourself by accepting the fact that other people around will have to do their own learning and make their own mistakes. Stand back and simply don't let your insides get so involved as they used to. Just relax, keep calm. Take a slow deep breath, exhale slowly.'

One can enhance one's sense of relaxation by imagining pleasant, peaceful scenes—although this technique must only be used in an appropriate situation (in the dentist's chair, for instance, not while driving a car!).

Learning to relax is an important feature in many forms of stress-management techniques, such as systematic desensitization and stress-inoculation training. In both these procedures, individuals who are anxious and fearful are asked to relax by means of exercises in which muscle groups are progressively tensed and relaxed. They are then asked to imagine a series of threatening scenes, from least fearful to most fearful. In this way, stressed individuals develop a visual image of how they will handle a potentially difficult situation effectively.

While relaxed, stressed people can thus use imagery or mental rehearsal to anticipate the real problems that they are likely to encounter. They can then break these into parts, or mini-stress events, and think of ways to handle each of them. For example, if one has to ask one's boss for a salary increase, and this turns out to be a stressful situation, think of a variety of scenarios and develop contingency plans for each one. At the end of this chapter is an addendum that illustrates one way in which relaxation skills are taught.

Decide what is important

Keep in mind that people who see stress as a challenge
or as a problem to be solved tend to think about *what*
they will do in the situation, while the stress-prone or
vulnerable tend to dwell on *how* they will do in the
situation. Faced with the need to take several urgent
decisions on different matters, for example, it is well
worth listing the likely consequences of *not* making a
decision. At least you are dealing with the realities of
the situation, rather than imagined catastrophes.

A list of likely real consequences, whether of action
or inaction, is the first step to establishing a system of

priorities. By making the list, you have accepted that your actions will affect the real world around you. You must then decide in what order the decisions should be made, whether you will be able to take them all by yourself, or whether you will need help from other people. Measuring these factors against a realistic estimate of the time available will help you decide in which order to tackle the problems. Extensive research into decision-making shows that specifying priorities, managing time, delegating authority and sharing responsibilities all help to reduce stress levels. By deciding *what* is to be done, you are well on the way to resolving *how* you are going to do it.

Rally your support systems

A major factor in the coping process is the degree of social support available to individuals. As the song says, 'With a little help from my friends' (whether the friend be a secretary, acquaintance, a relative, or even a group with which one identifies) stress may be reduced or avoided altogether.

Take a moment to list the people to whom you could turn in a crisis or stress. What is their relationship with you? Are they relatives, friends, neighbours, colleagues? How many of these people know each other? Do your support systems overlap, or do you have different support systems for different types of stress? Research suggests that individuals who cope most effectively tend to have a variety of support systems.

Such support systems fulfil a number of stress-reducing functions. One can find meaning in a crisis by sharing one's feelings with others; or, when stressed, one can seek aid and comfort. For example, if one is going to ask the boss for a raise, it is useful to ask others how they handled the situation. Support systems can provide much-needed information as well as feedback.

A major way of coping with stress is to know how to use others constructively. 'Constructive use' refers to the need to ensure that we do not abuse the good nature of others, but that instead we take the time and effort to adopt the other's perspective or viewpoint towards our request for help. Question yourself about how you would feel if someone asked you for help in this particular manner at this particular time. As the old adage says, 'One can go to the well once too often' and thus turn off the help that is sought. How is someone else likely to look upon your request for help? Questions like this will ensure that you will nurture your already existing support systems and develop new ones.

Keep communicating

The ability to listen, relate, share feelings and stand up for one's rights without being seen as pushy or aggressive is an important social skill which can help people to avoid and reduce stress. In the last few years, a number of books and programmes designed to help individuals improve these social skills have appeared. For example, Marsha Linehan and Kelly Egan's book, *Asserting yourself*, in this series, discusses the specific ways in which communication and assertive skills can be developed.

The ability to state requests clearly, to identify problems and to communicate needs plays an important role in reducing stress. People should be able to convey what is upsetting them or what they find stressful. An 'X-Y-Z' type of communication often helps, namely: 'When you do X in situation Y, it makes me feel Z. Did you realize that it made me feel that way? What can we do about that?' Direct communication along these lines often provides the basis for changing the situation, whereas a personal attack—'There you go again, you did it again. You're just like your father'—tends to be viewed as a personal challenge and to escalate the stress.

A good deal of stress takes the form of friction with others, and often the ways in which we communicate play an important role in contributing to it. For example, consider the couple who react to each other in an accusatory fashion, using expressions that put down the other without conveying exactly what it is that is so upsetting. 'You know, when you do that, you're just like your mother.' 'Well, what makes you think you're so perfect?' And so the battle rages, and the stress increases. As long as we view interpersonal conflicts as problems to be solved rather than as personal threats or provocations, we can avoid and reduce stress.

Adopt a problem-solving approach

How we view stressful events and our ability to cope with them is critical in determining the stress we experience. If we can think about events in a step-by-step fashion, we will be much more likely to avoid stress. The following steps have been suggested as a means of coping with stress:

1 Define the problem clearly in behavioural terms;

2 Generate a wide range of possible alternative courses of action;

3 Imagine and consider how others might respond if asked to solve a similar problem (e.g., how might your spouse approach this problem?);

4 Evaluate the pros and cons of each proposed solution, and rank them from least to most practicable and desirable;

5 Try out the most acceptable and feasible solution;

6 Reconsider the original problem in the light of this attempt at problem-solving. (Does the problem look different? Can you see anything positive about the situation?)

Adopting a problem-solving method of this kind involves: talking to people in order to obtain information; recalling things we have done before that required similar skills; imagining how someone else might cope; dividing stressful events into smaller manageable tasks; thinking of what lies ahead and making contingency plans; mentally rehearsing ways to handle each mini-stress; practising coping by rehearsing skills; looking to support systems for advice and support; gradually exposing oneself to small amounts of stress before entering high-pressure situations, thus boosting one's emotional defences; using coping skills but not 'catastrophizing' if things don't work out.

Failures or disappointments should be viewed as necessary feedback to help the problem-solving process to resume. The experiments that fail teach scientists the most. Each time we try to cope and fail, we probably say to ourselves, 'It doesn't work!' But we should use this occasion to ask what the 'it' is and what 'doesn't work' means. Are we saying that our efforts at coping will never work? Exactly what did we try in what situation? Did we fail because we did not have the skills, or did we fail because our thoughts and feelings got in the way of success? What evidence would prove that our efforts to cope had worked? Have we set too high a standard? Self-examination of this kind will help us avoid 'catastrophizing' and 'awfulizing' thoughts, and will reduce our stress level.

Ventilate your feelings

The ability to let off steam or relieve tension now and again seems to help people to cope with stress. We can express our feelings and unwind in many different ways, for instance by sharing our feelings with other people whom we know and trust, but who will not necessarily agree with us blindly. Other people may find that a more physically active form of expression helps, such as exercise or dancing. Having the capacity to laugh at ourselves now and then allows us to relax and enjoy ourselves. It is not a matter of having an emotional discharge such as screaming and yelling, but rather of using socially acceptable ways of expressing feelings and controlling reactions.

Such activities provide much-needed healing time, especially when severe stress has been experienced. Sometimes tranquillizing drugs, taken under doctor's orders, can facilitate the healing process. While the drugs themselves do not solve the problems, they may reduce the emotional reaction and thus permit a more level-headed problem-solving approach to be used in stressful situations.

Finally, there may be times when not doing anything or not thinking about the problem may be the best course of action to avoid and reduce stress. When there is nothing else to do, we might opt to deal with the problem by not thinking about it, especially when no dire consequences will follow from inaction.

The hell with coping –
It's more FUN
To lose my temper..

Addendum: relaxation training

When people become tense and uptight, when they are stressed, they usually feel it physically. Their heart rate goes up, their blood pressure climbs, they breathe more deeply and more rapidly and their muscles become tense. This exercise focuses on the muscles of the upper portion of the body, using controlled breathing. (Most relaxation training involves all body muscle groups.)

First, make yourself as comfortable as possible in the chair. Let the chair support your body totally. Loosen tight clothing. Remove your spectacles, close your eyes and take a moment to become as relaxed as possible.

Let us begin with the muscles of the hands. Make a fist with both the right and left hands. Feel the pull across the top and bottom of the hands. This is what is meant by tenseness. Hold it, and feel the sensations in your hands. Let your fingers come away from your palms slowly; separate your fingers a little and gradually rest them on the arm of the chair. Feel the changes; notice your hands, how the tension begins to disappear and the tightness slowly fades. You become aware of a sense of calm relaxation. Note that your hands are becoming more and more relaxed and that a sense of warmth and calm is spreading through the muscles of your hands. Notice the changes you are bringing about.

Now that you have relaxed the muscles of both hands, tense and hold the muscles of your chest and back. Do this by filling your lungs slowly, with short deep breaths, holding each one and then slowly breathing out. Hold your breath until you feel the need to exhale. Part your lips slightly and breathe out. Let the air out so that your chest assumes its normal position. Continue to breathe evenly and easily.

Now try to inhale fully and then exhale slowly. In order to control how fast you exhale, just imagine you are blowing across the top of a spoon of hot soup, gently so that you don't spill it, or that you are flickering a candle without blowing it out. Notice the difference between the states of tension and relaxation.

Some people have found that they can enhance their state of relaxation even further by saying to themselves 'relax', 'calm' as they exhale. You may even be able to see the letters R-E-L-A-X or C-A-L-M in your mind's eye. Other people find it helpful to picture a calm, peaceful scene as they exhale. Think of some moment when you were relaxed and carefree, or imagine a pleasant scene.

The use of slow, deep breathing is an excellent way to short-circuit the effects of stress. You can control how you feel; you can interrupt the cycle of tension and bring about a state of calm. Then you can begin to use the other coping responses we have discussed. When you are calm, it is easier to see stressful events as problems to be solved than as personal threats.

Use slow deep breathing whenever you feel the early signs of stress. Learning to relax is a skill that has to be acquired like any other skill. It requires practice but it pays handsome dividends.

There are, of course, many different ways of relaxing, and it is not clear that any one way is better than any other. Find a way that is comfortable for you, a way in which you have some confidence. Then practise it and try out the procedures in stressful situations.

7

Treating stress disorders

If you can keep your head when all about you
Are losing theirs and blaming it on you . . .

RUDYARD KIPLING (1865–1936)

What can be done to reduce and avoid stress in individuals, groups and society? We begin with a consideration of stress disorders in combat, since most of the information about treating stress disorders comes from research on and clinical work with soldiers.

Treating combat stress

In 1883 the Surgeon-General of the Union Army in the USA described what he called 'nostalgia', a debilitating psychological reaction to combat. During the First World War, this same condition was called 'shell shock', in the Second World War 'combat fatigue', and in the Korean and Vietnam wars it became known as 'stress disorders'. The combat stress reaction may include non-specific anxiety, specific fears, depression, fatigue and nightmares. Experience has brought increasingly effective treatment. During the Second World War, the proportion of soldiers relieved of duty due to stress disorders was 101 per 1 000, during the Korean War 37 per 1 000, and during the Vietnam War 12 per 1 000.

What accounts for this improvement is a changed attitude and approach to treatment. Three concepts characterize the present approach. The first is immediacy: the goal is early detection of soldiers who are showing signs of stress and their quick removal from combat for treatment. Second is proximity: treatment is offered as near the combat unit and the battle zone as possible. Stressed individuals can thus be reunited with their buddies as soon as possible. The third guiding concept is the expectancy that the soldier will return to his or her combat unit with a role to perform and that the stress-reaction will not lead to an 'easy way out'. Treatment is so arranged that avoidance or special benefits (technically called 'secondary gains') are unlikely to occur.

Treatment in the combat zone usually consists of rest, sleep, adequate food, the chance to bath, shave and so forth, and an opportunity to discuss one's

experiences. Reassuring therapy is combined with proper rest, often supplemented with mild sedatives. Stressed individuals such as soldiers benefit from the opportunity to 'ventilate', that is, to express their emotions and thoughts to a listener or to a group of other soldiers. They share their grief and stress in this way. Repetitive talking about stressful experiences and the expression of stress in the form of fantasies, dreams and nightmares often seem to act as a built-in repair mechanism. In extreme cases, the stressed individual is given an injection of sodium pentothal. This helps the individual to relive the traumatic situation and thus permits an emotional discharge, which is followed by an opportunity to discuss the stress reaction.

The combat-zone treatment of stress reactions has generally proved quite successful, and approximately 80 to 90 per cent of stressed soldiers return to combat; of these only about 10 per cent break down a second time. As noted earlier, however, in a minority of cases combat stress may have residual effects well after discharge.

perhaps
a LITTLE...

A number of studies have tried to determine which soldiers are most vulnerable to stress. One study of British soldiers in the Second World War showed that psychiatric casualties tended to be 'worriers, pessimistic, moody, sexually inhibited and inadequate men' before they joined the army. Of the stressed soldiers who were hospitalized, 40 per cent revealed abnormalities in early personality development (e.g. disruptive home environment, poverty, alcoholism or family discord). Those soldiers who broke down under a relatively minor degree of stress had the strongest predisposing factors and the poorest response to treatment. Those soldiers who had a more favourable predisposition and background endured more severe stressful conditions and, if they did break down, showed a more positive outcome.

Thus some individuals seem less vulnerable and better equipped to handle stress, while others are more vulnerable to stress. If we could identify such highly vulnerable individuals, not only in combat but also in civilian life, then we could begin to develop programmes to train or 'inoculate' them from stress.

..TINY BIT of ANXIETY...

We could also consider engineering environments so that such vulnerable groups experience less stress.

Stress-inoculation training

The idea of providing an individual with a defence against stress is in some respects analogous to inoculation against disease. The general underlying principle is that a person's resistance is enhanced by exposure to a stimulus strong enough to arouse the defences without being so powerful as to overcome the individual.

At the University of Waterloo in Ontario, my colleagues (Roy Cameron, Myles Genest and Dennis Turk) and I have developed a stress-inoculation training programme, to be used on both a preventative and a treatment basis, which has been successful with a variety of groups, including anxious and phobic patients, patients who have trouble with anger control, pain and burn patients, rape victims and

alcoholics. Recently, the programme has been extended on a preventative basis to surgical patients, patients preparing for noxious medical examination, law enforcement officers, and members of the armed services, among others. Although a good deal more research is needed to determine the efficacy of the programme, it is worth looking at it in detail.

What is involved?

Stress-inoculation training can last as little as one hour, in the case of patients about to undergo surgery, for instance, to as many as 40 sessions when severely disturbed psychiatric patients are being treated. Obviously, the way in which the treatment is conducted varies according to its length. Treatment can be either on an individual or on a group basis. Trainers include professionals (psychiatrists, psychologists, social workers) and non-professionals (police officers, soldiers, and so forth).

As the name of the training implies, individuals are

provided with defences, or sets of skills to enable them to deal with stressful situations. The programme usually involves three phases. The first is designed to develop a better understanding of the nature of an individual's stress response. The second teaches specific coping skills or ensures that the coping skills someone already possesses are in fact used; many individuals do not cope simply because they lack the necessary skills to do so. The final phase is designed to provide graded practice, so the various coping skills can be tried out.

The general principles of stress-inoculation training involve teaching or encouraging individuals to consider what lies ahead; to split stressful events into manageable doses; to think of ways to handle each mini-stress; and to practise coping skills. More specifically, the training is designed to help individuals:

1 To discover that others often have similar problems and what they do to solve them;

2 To understand more about how thinking, feeling and behaving are related;

3 To learn to approach problems in a step-by-step manner in order to avoid feeling overwhelmed;

4 To ensure that they have adequate coping skills (problem-solving, relaxation, time-management, the use of social supports, communication and assertive skills);

5 To experiment with and practise their coping skills systematically.

Many of the skills described in the last chapter are included in the stress-inoculation training procedure. For example, an individual may be asked to describe situations in which he or she experiences stress and then to relive the situation through imagery—that is, through replaying in slow motion the thoughts and feelings that preceded, accompanied and followed the stressful situation. This helps him or her to understand the ways in which stress levels are self-manufactured. The individual then considers other situations in which similar thoughts and feelings are experienced and searches for common factors. The trainer helps the individual to realize the impact of hidden agenda, current concerns, catastrophizing thoughts and images on the stressful reaction.

Breaking the problem down

If such thoughts and feelings do engender stress, then trainer and patient can work together to formulate problem-solving strategies. The stressful event is recreated by being broken into a sequence of several phases. The sequences include preparation for the stress; confronting and handling it; coping with feelings of being overwhelmed; and, finally, reflection on how the situation was handled. The trainer works with the patient so that he or she becomes aware of thoughts and feelings that may add to the stress reaction during each of these four phases. Together, the patient and trainer generate a list of alternative strategies to handle stressful events.

The trainer also encourages patients to employ whatever coping techniques they may already possess, and provides a variety of other direct action and cognitive coping techniques. Direct action techniques include collecting information, changing the environment in some way, arranging escape routes, learning physical and mental relaxation skills, communication skills, and so forth. Cognitive coping techniques include training in the fundamentals of problem-solving, altering appraisals, shifting attention, imagery, rehearsal, etc.

Patients are encouraged to use such coping strategies before, during and after a stressful situation. The stressful event of trying to control one's fear or one's anger can be broken down into various phases. These are: the period before the actual stress begins; actual confrontation with the stress; handling one's own intense reactions; and reflecting on how things went.

At each of these phases we can use a number of strategies to control how we react. There are things we can do and say to ourselves that will influence how stressed we become. We are not the mere victims of stress, but can influence our reactions.

The suggestions offered in Tables B and C provide examples of how one might cope with situations which arouse fear or anger. Similar coping strategies can be developed for other upsetting events, such as depression and anxiety. It is important to understand that it is not being suggested that the experience of fear, anger or any other negative emotion *per se* is bad, but that these emotions should be expressed in a socially appropriate fashion.

Table B
Coping with a fear or a phobia

Preparing for fear

What do I have to do?
I can develop a plan to deal with it.
I must concentrate on what I can do about it. That's better than getting anxious.
No negative statements about myself; I must think rationally.
I must not worry; worry won't help me.
Maybe what I think is anxiety is really eagerness to confront my fear.

Confronting fear

I must 'psych' myself up—I can meet this challenge.
I can do it. I can reason fear away.
One step at a time: I can handle the situation.
I mustn't think about fear, just about what I have to do.
I mustn't let my attention wander.
This anxiety is what the doctor said I might feel.
It's a reminder to use my coping exercises.
This tenseness can be an ally, a cue to cope.
Relax. I'm in control. Take a slow, deep breath. Ah, good.

(continues overleaf)

121

Coping with fearful feelings

Here comes the fear. Pause.
Keep focusing on the present: what is it I have to do?
I'm going to label my fear from 0 to 10 and watch it change.
I can expect my fear to rise.
I won't try to eliminate my fear totally, just to keep it manageable.

Reflection

It worked. I did it.
Wait until I tell my therapist (or group) about this.
It wasn't as bad as I expected.
I made more out of my fear than it was worth.
My damned ideas—that's the problem. When I control them, I can control my fear.
It's getting better each time I use the procedure.
I feel pleased at the progress I'm making.
I did it.

Table C
Coping with anger

Preparing for anger

This could be a rough situation, but I know how to deal with it.

I can work out a plan to handle this. Easy does it.

Remember, stick to the issues and don't take things personally.

There won't be any need for an argument. I know what to do.

Confronting anger

As long as I keep my cool I'll be in control of the situation.

I don't need to prove myself, and I mustn't make more out of this than I have to.

There's no point in getting mad. Concentrate on what has to be done.

Look for the positives and don't jump to conclusions.

Coping with angry feelings

My muscles are tensing up. Relax. Slow things down.

Take a deep breath. Now let's go through this point by point.

My anger is a signal telling me what I need to do: it's problem-solving time.

He probably wants and expects me to get angry, but I won't. I'm going to deal with this constructively.

Reflection: conflict unresolved

Forget it. Thinking about it only makes me upset.

Try to shake it off. Don't let it interfere with the things I do well.

Relax. It's a lot better than getting angry.

Don't take it personally. It's not so serious.

(*continues overleaf*)

Reflection: conflict resolved

I handled that one pretty well. That's good!
I could have got more upset, but it wasn't worth it.
My pride can get me into trouble, but I'm getting better at
   stopping myself getting into trouble.
I actually got through that without getting angry.
I can keep my cool.

These suggestions are designed to encourage individuals to express their feelings constructively rather than destructively. As long as we view stressful events as problems to be solved rather than as personal threats or provocations, we increase the likelihood of our being able to cope with stress.

The goal of stress-inoculation training is to teach people to become sensitive to the preliminary signs of stress (thoughts, feelings and behavioural and physiological reactions) and then to interrupt the cycle and use the coping skills developed in training. However, coping skills must be practised so that a sense of self-confidence is built up.

A case study

Ray Novaco has offered an interesting case study of an individual treated by means of stress-inoculation training. The client was Tom, a 38-year-old credit manager for a national firm, who had been hospitalized because he was depressed, feeling worthless and inadequate, and was even considering suicide. He had been under considerable job pressure and had developed headaches and chest pains. He was married and had six children, one of whom had been diagnosed as hyperactive.

Clinical interviews revealed that Tom had a great deal of anger and hostility toward his colleagues and supervisors, even though he bottled it up and reacted in an over-controlled fashion. He would actively suppress his anger and would periodically explode in verbal fireworks. At home, he was intolerant and easily provoked. The children's fights frequently elicited anger, which he readily expressed both verbally and physically. As he stated, he was reacting 'out of proportion' and felt helpless.

During hospitalization, stress-inoculation training was conducted three times a week for three and a half weeks, and follow-up sessions were conducted twice weekly for two months. The initial phase of treatment focused on making Tom aware of his personal anger pattern and the functions of anger (i.e. what causes anger and how anger can be regulated). The discussion focused on such topics as (a) recognizing the first signs of tension and arousal; (b) identifying persons and situations that triggered anger; (c) discriminating between justified and unnecessary anger; (d) appreciating the transactional model of stress.

The second phase was devoted to learning and rehearsing coping skills. Tom was taught how to view situations in terms of problems to be solved rather than as personal threats. The method was to encourage Tom to identify what he wanted the result of the situation to be, then to list the best possible

How to recognise a stressed person...

approaches to achieving the desired outcome. Tom also found it helpful to practise relaxation, maintaining a sense of humour, taking the other person's perspective, and communicating his feelings effectively but without stridency.

During the final phase, Tom underwent graded doses of anger stimuli by means of imagery and role-playing. He was asked to imagine a series of scenes ranging from those least likely to provoke anger to those which, in the past, had driven him into frenzies of fury and frustration. While imagining these scenes, Tom mentally rehearsed the various anger control skills he had already developed. Later, these scenes were actually played out, with Tom and the therapist taking opposing roles. Finally, Tom was encouraged to use his anger control coping skills in real life, initially in relatively safe situations and then, with practice, in more demanding social situations.

The treatment proved successful in helping Tom to deal with his anger and to reduce his accompanying depression. For example, he found it much easier to control his irritation with his children, even though there were many highly provocative incidents. At work, too, he was much better able to express his feelings in a constructive manner.

Stress-inoculation for groups

Although one must be careful in generalizing from a given case study, Novaco's report on the potential value of stress-inoculation training has now been repeated in other cases, for instance with policemen.

The purpose of Ray Novaco's training of this particular group was to prepare policemen to encounter crisis and provocation. The training began with the policemen reviewing situations in which they became stressed and angry, and with Novaco helping them to distinguish between various kinds of provocation. These included: annoyance (a drunk being sick in the back of the squad car, for example); frustration (members of the public being uncooperative); ego-threat (being called names such as 'Pig', 'Superpig'); assault (being attacked by a suspect); inequities (being suspended for actions that were unavoidable in the circumstances).

Parenthetically it is interesting to note that a recent police study in Florida found that bureaucratic hassles (form-filling, unnecessary paperwork, poor relationships with supervisors) were rated as being among the severest sources of stress.

Novaco's discussion with the policemen of those situations which created the most stress led him to pinpoint certain personal and situational factors common to their feelings of stress, anger and aggression.

The 'short fuse' was a common personal factor. A policeman's reactions to a situation were often coloured by recent negative events, such as criticism from a superior or trouble with a police car. These rankled and played a critical role in influencing the degree of stress felt. Naturally the greater the stress, the less clearly one thinks about a problem.

In police work the situation is often the stressing factor. Some policemen, for example, reported getting very angry when called upon to deal with hippies. They strongly resented their slovenly clothes and unkempt hair. Clearly this resentment had a lot to do with personal standards. Here underlying personal factors come into play again.

Often an individual's reactions are influenced by cognitive determinants of a more permanent kind than recent criticism from a superior or annoying paperwork. Recollections, expectations and beliefs all colour a person's reaction to a situation. One police officer admitted that he was constantly seeking the approval of those around him. What did his fellow officers think of him? What did his supervisor think of him? For him, every encounter was a personal test. Another officer felt a strong need to be in control, not only in his police duties, but at home with his children, his wife and his friends. Whenever this need was violated he became very stressed.

Each one of us has our areas of vulnerability, our

own concerns which influence how we appraise situations. For some of us, stress is rooted in a need for social approval or in the need to feel in control. For others stress may spring from a desire to achieve, or from a strong sense of equity. In many of us none of these needs is paramount; they all, to some degree, compete in us. But if one feels under continual pressure then one must ask oneself: is there one need which, if thwarted, is more important than any of the others? Is there a need that causes stress across a lot of different situations? What are the precise thoughts and feelings that exacerbate the stress felt in a particular situation?

Returning to the policemen in Novaco's study, another factor that contributed to anger reactions was the manner in which policemen found themselves responding to perceived provocations. The knowledge, for example, that he is being unnecessarily tough with a suspect can escalate the stress an officer feels during an interrogation.

As a result of these analyses, the policemen developed a different view of their stress reactions. They saw that they were composed of an interdependent sequence of cognitive, affective, behavioural and physiological components triggered by specific provocations. With this knowledge they were encouraged to notice and keep track of when and why they became stressed and angry. They became aware of just how much and how often their own feelings, thoughts and actions contributed to their stress. They realized they were not the helpless victims of stress but contributors to it. They were encouraged to notice the build-up signs and to use a variety of coping skills to de-escalate that build-up.

The next step in Novaco's training was to ensure that policemen developed a flexible coping repertoire and a general plan for putting that repertoire into effect. They were encouraged to help each other generate and practise various coping skills. These included relaxation, self-defence, communication, negotiation, group organization, and so on. After practising each of these skills they would break into small groups and discuss situations in which such skills would be most helpful. For example, each officer would describe three stressful situations in vivid detail, and for each the group would examine the situational factors, the personal factors that made the stress worse or better, and the pros and cons of different coping strategies. Practical sessions followed, in which officers were asked to act out the situations they had described. In addition, they saw a film showing policemen successfully dealing with stressful situations, and were asked to re-enact them, modelling themselves on the behaviour shown in the film.

After discussing the modelling film the policemen practised what they had seen first in role play, then in real life. Role playing offers a safe environment in which to assess and fine tune one's coping competence. Initially role play scenarios are less provoking and intense than in real life, but as skill and confidence increase they become more and more stressful. At one point, in Novaco's training, actors dressed up as taunting hippies. As Novaco noted, the actors 'directly challenged the officers' manhood, questioned their maternal ancestry, or remarked on their spouses' occupation' most convincingly! Role play was followed by supportive and corrective feedback, some of it on videotape.

Equipped with the necessary coping skills, the policemen moved on to real life situations, graduating from the least to the most provocative.

Although in this instance stress reduction was brought about by the development of more adaptive coping skills, there are, in any stressful climate, other levels of intervention that can and should be considered. In the case of the police, could stress be reduced by changing the organizational constraints under which the police work? Could the social environment in which they work be changed?

The difficulties of attempting to change entrenched organizational practices and attitudes should not be underestimated. In some cases change can be brought about by providing feedback and constructive alternatives; in others change can only be achieved by mobilizing group pressure. The important point is that efforts to reduce stress may need to take place at the institutional or organizational level as well as at the level of the individual.

Non-professional help

The sources of help we most naturally turn to in times of stress are of course family, friends and neighbours, and at one time or another we have all found ourselves trying to console someone or to reduce their stress reactions, in some instances by 'just being there'.

Research indicates that we should be cautious in providing such help. For example, interviews with widows indicated that, when friends tried to comfort them with such comments as 'Don't worry, you're young, you can marry again', or 'You're attractive, you will have no problem finding someone else', they felt even more upset and stressed.

Similarly, we can learn from those parents who have experienced the sudden unexplained death of their infant (a disease called Sudden Infant Death Syndrome, or SIDS). Two psychologists, Roxanne Silver and Camille Wortman, have studied SIDS parents and have noted how such parents react to their relatives' and friends' attempts to help them. SIDS parents reacted badly to efforts to comfort them when their comforter's comments included remarks about 'having another child', or suggestions that the baby 'was so young that they couldn't really have developed a strong attachment', and so forth. Victims rarely find such 'moving on' statements comforting or stress-reducing.

Instead, SIDS parents reported that they had found it much more helpful to discuss with other SIDS parents the details of the stressful episode (hospital, death, and so forth), as well as their expectations and fantasies about their child. In most instances, friends and families tended to avoid these topics and often tried to shift the focus of the discussion, whereas the parents found it useful to express their feelings. Helpers must be sensitive to the concerns of the victims and follow their lead.

Well-meaning advice: give with care

Another example of a loved one's efforts to help having just the opposite effect is offered by David Mechanic. Mechanic reported that when spouses of graduate students facing a crucial examination re-marked that 'I'm sure you'll pass', the student's stress level often increased. By contrast, comments to the effect that the student should 'do the best you can' were seen as much more supportive and helpful. In short, we should ensure that our efforts to help those who are stressed do not contribute to the problem we are trying to alleviate.

In helping others, it is important to permit victims and stressed individuals to develop their own meaning of the situation. One should be careful not to impose a meaning. Often the victim is responding to something that cannot be in the future, rather than to what has been lost.

In addition, the stressed individual may have thoughts and feelings of which the helper is unaware. For example, bereaved people may have visions of their deceased partner which they may be reluctant to share, for fear of what others may think. While perfectly natural, such thoughts and feelings may engender more stress in the victim. The bereaved person not only has to cope with the death of the partner, but also with his own reactions and with increasing concern about how others will respond. Admonitions that the partner will soon be forgotten or that it was 'all for the best' may exacerbate the stressful situation. The victim's current concerns and hidden agenda may not be readily available, and we should keep this in mind when we try to provide comfort and help.

A similar story can be told about cancer patients who often find that their condition causes family, friends and employers to draw away from them, causing additional stress. We should ask ourselves: 'Are we really being helpful or can our efforts have just the opposite effect?'

Helpers must be cautious not to impose their expectation of how the individual should react or cope. Keep in mind the various myths we discussed earlier about the nature of coping. The coping response of stressed individuals varies markedly, and there is no set series of reactions through which individuals must go in order to cope. Coping is a complex process; there is no one fixed way to cope with stress.

In time, some—though not all—of us, when under stress, may wish to 'ventilate' or share our feelings and discuss our reactions. Similarly, at some point, we may be encouraged to begin to view the stressful situation as a problem to be solved rather than as a personal threat, or a provocation, or as the 'end of the world'. The adoption of a problem-solving attitude and the accompanying step-by-step thought processes really can help us to come to terms with the situation.

Several recent stress-reduction programmes have capitalized on the value of one-to-one contacts. In one recent project, widows were trained to become widow-aides providing support for the newly bereaved. The widow-aides acted as models or examples for the bereaved, supplying evidence that someone who has been similarly distressed has coped and has put her life together once again.

Help may also take the form of crisis-intervention services. Their number is increasing, and includes drop-in centres, telephone hot-lines, non-professional groups such as groups for single parents, child-abusers, alcoholics, overweight people, and so forth.

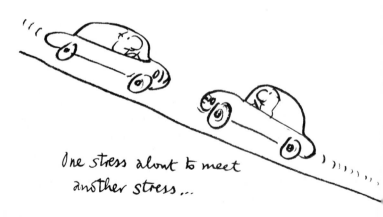

One stress about to meet
another stress...

The group as a support system

The group is an important resource for helping people to cope with stress. Identification with a group can play a significant role in reducing stress. As noted earlier, people tend to manifest less stress or fear in the presence of others than when left alone. Courage and heroism often grow out of group cohesiveness, a sense of mutual responsibility and group morale. The sentiment 'I did it for my friends because I was convinced they would have done the same for me' reflects the way in which the group can help individuals to cope with stress. In the armed forces, the sense of commitment to the combat unit and the desire to maintain group cohesiveness contribute to combat gallantry.

In one study of new military recruits, the degree of stress in training camp was found to be closely related to the group morale of each platoon. Feelings of camaraderie, social bonds, the sense of relief that follows from learning that others also feel scared, nervous, worried and angry and from realizing that one is not alone in being criticized—all these contributed to the coping process. By sharing experiences with members of the group, the recruits developed a more adaptive perspective. The knowledge that other recruits have felt similarly distressed, but did somehow successfully complete their training, is both reassuring and stress-reducing. Teamwork, and competition between individual platoons, also contributed to group identity, to a sense of group pride or *esprit de corps* and to a sense of togetherness that encouraged recruits to support and inspire one another.

In helping individuals to cope with stress, we should consider how we can engineer events so that supportive groups are formed. Our objective should be to form social support systems or groups that provide individuals with information that leads them to feel that they are cared for, esteemed and a member of a network of mutual obligations.

The importance of group structure in affecting levels of stress has been indicated by Ofra Ayalon's analysis of how various communities in Israel responded to terrorist attacks. Like individuals, communities vary in their vulnerability to stress. Israeli communities were distinguished in terms of their size, cohesiveness, leadership, preparedness to meet attacks (through prior drill, effective role allocation and communication), the speed of their recovery, and the degree to which a framework of traditional and religious values existed that enabled people to work through their grief.

When support becomes pressure

While groups can act as a resource to help people to cope with stress, at certain times group pressures to conform or group expectations can actually cause stress. In addition, the group decision-making process can sometimes interfere with problem-solving aimed at coping.

Two psychologists, Irving Janis and Leo Mann, have described two patterns of group behaviour that contribute to defective decision-making: these are defensive avoidance and hyper-vigilance. Defensive avoidance means that the group tries to seek relief from emotional tension by engaging in 'wishful thinking', using reassuring illusions or rationalizations and distorting the likelihood of certain dangers. Group members may assert feelings of solidarity and avoid debating controversial issues that could upset the group atmosphere. If someone does argue against the group's shared view of things, the group will often put pressure on him or her to conform to the group norm or will simply ignore him or her. Group coherence of this kind often leads to the belief that there is no need to worry about excessive risks.

Hyper-vigilance is an attempt on the part of the group to avoid the stress caused by disagreement by racing through the agenda at frenetic speed. Problems are examined superficially and hurriedly: decisions are made impulsively amid an atmosphere of growing panic. In these conditions, the group's anxiety to preserve its own cohesion prevents it from dealing effectively with the real problems it is there to consider.

Political scientists and psychologists have studied the group decision-making processes surrounding such events as the Bay of Pigs invasion of Cuba by the USA, decisions during the Vietnam War, and other similar events. In each case, instances of defensive avoidance and hyper-vigilance in the group process engendered stress and contributed to faulty decisions.

Yet vigilance—the group's awareness of itself—can be used constructively. By recognizing stress the group can identify genuine issues of disagreement which must be resolved before the group can continue with the decision-making process. In this climate, individuals within the group are more likely to remain alert to problems, to search for relevant information, to weigh consequences carefully, and to avoid panicky decisions.

Insurance against stress

In most instances, individuals and groups do not react with panic, even when traumatic stressful events such as floods, hurricanes and so forth occur. Panic reactions usually occur when the group feels directly threatened, when there is no pre-arranged plan of how to deal with the situation, and when there appears to be only one line of escape that may be only momentarily available (e.g., one exit in a theatre where a fire has broken out). If we recognize that these conditions lead individuals and groups to panic, then as a society we should anticipate such occurrences as much as possible and create stress-reducing environments. Social planners, architects and others are becoming more sensitive to the ways in which the environment can be engineered to reduce stress. Noise-abatement programmes, active concern about population density and pollution, and the development of recreational areas are just some examples of how a society goes about insuring itself against stress.

The environmental psychologist is a new phenomenon, but he or she is being listened to as never before. By engineering our environment we can work to avoid and reduce stress.

Managing stress through social rituals

Every society has established rituals or socially accepted practices that help individuals to cope with stress. For example, mourning rituals such as funerals and wakes can ease the burden of stress that accompanies the death of a family member. Religious services can provide helpful perspectives and comfort at troubling times. Every society possesses certain norms, beliefs and customs concerning the appropriate behaviour to be displayed during mourning. Such practices usually provide support for the bereaved by allowing a recognized period of withdrawal and by setting a schedule for the reorganization of behaviour.

The social milieu can engender or reduce individual stress in many other instances. The psychologist Rudolph Moos has produced a number of questionnaires assessing the social climate of a particular setting. These indicate the degree of autonomy fostered; the extent to which people are involved in decisions and how much they help and support one another; how far free and spontaneous expression is encouraged; and how orderly the environment is.

Moos has reported that environments low in involvement, support and autonomy and high in competition, strictness and control tend to engender stress. This stress is evident in frequent complaints of physical symptoms, high rates of sick leave, absenteeism, high job turnover and high drop-out rates. These results hold up whether the social milieu is a work area, a psychiatric hospital, a prison, or a university.

For example, imagine your own place of work. How

would you describe this setting in terms of the amount of (a) worker participation in decision-making; (b) help and support from fellow-workers; (c) order or degree of structure of the job, and so forth? The social climate of the work-place can play an important role in influencing the amount of stress one experiences.

Work of this kind on social climates indicates that, if we wish to understand the nature of stress and coping, we should focus our attention not only on the individual but also on the social climate and on social practices and expectations. For example, rape victims often report that their stress is compounded by the attitudes and treatment they encounter from the helping professions, from members of the legal and medical professions, as well as from the police. One should therefore, as well as helping rape victims directly, work to change the attitudes of these social groups. Efforts to reduce stress should be multi-levelled.

While we should recognize that we are not victims of stress, we should also realize that individual efforts to cope are not substitutes for social change, especially where structural social problems are present. We can reduce and avoid stress by teaching better coping skills; by raising self-esteem; by helping people to identify and establish support groups; and also by reducing preventable and unnecessary forms of stress. In this way, we will enhance the quality of life.

References

Chapter 1

Csilszentimhalyi, M., *Flow: Studies of Enjoyment.* Chicago: University of Chicago, 1974

Dohrenwend, B. and Dohrenwend, B. (eds), *Stressful Life Events: Their Nature and Effects.* New York: Wiley, 1974

Gleser, G., Green, B. and Winget, C., *Prolonged Psychosocial Effects of Disaster: A Study of Buffalo Creek.* New York: Academic Press, 1981

Guntern, G., *Social Change, Stress, and Mental Health in the Pearl of the Alps.* New York: Springer-Verlag, 1979

Johnson, J. and Sarason, J., Recent developments in research on life stress. In: Hamilton, V. and Warburton, D. (eds), *Human Stress and Cognition: An Information Processing Approach.* New York: Wiley, 1979

Lazarus, R., *Psychological Stress and the Coping Process.* New York: McGraw-Hill, 1966

Sarason, I., Johnson, J. and Siegel, J., Assessing the impact of life changes: development of the Life Experiences Survey. *Journal of Consulting and Clinical Psychology*, 1978, 46, 932–46

Selye, H., *Stress without Distress.* Philadelphia: Lippincott, 1974

Chapter 2

Burgess, A. and Holmstrom, L., *Rape: Victims of Crisis.* Bowie, Maryland: Robert Brady, 1974

Ellis, A., What people can do for themselves to cope with stress. In: Cooper, C. and Payne, R. (eds), *Stress at Work*. New York: Wiley, 1978

Janoff-Bulman, R., Characterological versus behavioral self-blame: inquiries into depression and rape. *Journal of Personality and Social Psychology*, 1979, *37*, 1798–1809

Janoff-Bulman, R. and Wortman, C., Attributions of blame and coping in the 'Real World': severe accident victims react to their lot. *Journal of Personality and Social Psychology*, 1977, *35*, 351–63

Lazarus, R. and Averill, J., Emotion and cognition: with special reference to anxiety. In: Spielberger, C. (ed.), *Anxiety: Current Trends in Theory and Research*, vol 2. New York: Academic Press, 1972

Mahoney, M. and Avener, M., Psychology of the elite athlete: an exploratory study. *Cognitive Therapy and Research*, 1977, *1*, 135–42

Meichenbaum, D., Henshaw, D. and Himel, N., Coping with stress as a problem-solving process. In: Krohne, W. and Laux, L. (eds), *Achievement, Stress and Anxiety*. Washington, D.C.: Hemisphere Press, 1982

Chapter 3

Bowers, K. and Kelley, P., Stress, disease, psychotherapy and hypnosis. *Journal of Abnormal Psychology*, 1979, *88*, 490–505

Cannon, W., *The Wisdom of the Body*. New York: Norton, 1932

Dewe, P., Guest, D. and Williams, R., Methods of coping with work-related stress. In: Mackay, I. C. and Cox, T. (eds), *Response to Stress: Occupational Aspects.* London: IPC and Technology Press, 1979

Frankenhaeuser, M., Psychoneuroendocrine approaches to the study of emotion as related to stress and coping. In: Dienstbier, R. (ed.), *1978 Nebraska Symposium on Motivation.* Lincoln, Nebraska: University of Nebraska Press, 1979

Friedman, M. and Rosenman, R., *Type A Behavior and Your Heart.* Greenwich, Connecticut: Fawcett Publications, 1974

Glass, D., *Behavior Patterns, Stress and Coronary Disease.* Hillsdale, New Jersey: Lawrence Erlbaum Associates, 1977

Haggerty, K., Changing lifestyles to improve health. *Preventive Medicine,* 1977, 6, 276–89

Horowitz, M., *Stress Responses Syndrome.* New York: Aronson, 1976

Horowitz, M., Psychological responses to serious life events. In: Hamilton, V. and Warburton, D. (eds), *Human Stress and Cognition: An Information Processing Approach.* New York: Wiley, 1979

Kubler-Ross, E., *On Death and Dying.* New York: Macmillan, 1969

Lewandowski, A., An investigation of the cognitive and attitudinal correlates of coronary prone behaviour pattern. Unpublished doctoral dissertation, University of Waterloo, Waterloo, Ontario, 1979

Mason, J., Specificity in the organization of neuro-endocrine response profiles. In: Seeman, P. and Brown, J. (eds), *Frontiers in Neurology and Neuroscience Research*. Toronto, Ontario: University of Toronto Press, 1974

Mason, J., A historical view of the stress field. *Journal of Human Stress*, 1975, *1*, 6–12

Mason, J., Emotion as reflected in patterns of endocrine integration. In: Levi, L. (ed.), *Emotions: Their Parameters and Measurement*. New York: Raven Press, 1975

Rabkin, J. and Struening, E., Life events, stress and illness. *Science*, 1896, *194*, 1013–20

Selye, H., The evolution of stress concept. *American Scientist*, 1973, *61*, 692–9

Selye, H., *The Stress of Life*, 2nd edition. New York: McGraw-Hill, 1978

Silver, R. and Wortman, C., Coping with undesirable Life Events. In: Garber, J. and Seligman, M. (eds), *Human Helplessness: Theory and Applications*. New York: Academic Press, 1980

Chapter 4

Antonovsky, A., *Health, Stress and Coping*. San Francisco: Jossey-Bass, 1979

Coelho, G., Hamburg, D. and Adams, J. (eds), *Coping and Adaptation*. New York: Basic Books, 1974

Cousins, N., Anatomy of an illness (as perceived by the patient). *New England Journal of Medicine*, 1976, *195*, 1458–63

Dimsdale, J., The coping behavior of Nazi concentration camp survivors. *American Journal of Psychiatry*, 1974, *131*, 792–7

Dimsdale, J., *The Holocaust: A Multidisciplinary Study.* Washington, D.C.: Hemisphere Press, 1980

Figley, C., *Stress Disorders among Vietnam Veterans: Theory, Research and Treatment.* New York: Brunner/Mazel, 1978

Janis, I., *Air War and Emotional Stress.* New York: McGraw-Hill, 1951

Lazarus, R. and Launier, R., Stress-related transactions between person and environment. In: Pervin, L. and Lewis, M. (eds), *Perspectives in Interactional Psychology.* New York: Plenum Press, 1978

May, R., *Man's Search for Himself.* New York: W. W. Norton, 1953

Mundey, J., Women. In: Bates, E. and Wilson, P. (eds), *Mental Disorder or Madness: Alternative Theories.* St Lucca, Queensland: University of Queensland Press, 1979

Pearlin, L. and Schooler, C., The structure of coping. *Journal of Health and Social Behavior*, 1978, *19*, 2–21

Rachman, S. J., *Fear and Courage.* San Francisco: W. H. Freeman, 1978

Ursin, H., Baade, E. and Levine, S., *Psychobiology of Stress: A Study of Coping Men.* New York: Academic Press, 1979

Visotsky, H., Gross, M. and Lebovits, B., Coping behavior under extreme stress. *Archives of General Psychiatry*, 1961, *5*, 432–48

Weisman, A., *Coping with Cancer*. New York: McGraw-Hill, 1979

Weisman, A. and Sobel, H., Coping with cancer through self-instruction: a hypothesis. *Journal of Human Stress*, 1979, *5*, 3–8

Chapter 5

Breznitz, S., A study of worrying. *British Journal of Social and Clinical Psychology*, 1871, *10*, 271–9

Cobb, S., Social support as a moderator of life stress. *Psychosomatic Medicine*, 1976, *38*, 300–14

Dean, A. and Lin, N., The stress-buffering role of social support: problems and prospects for systematic investigation. *Journal of Nervous and Mental Disease*, 1977, *165*, 403–17

Fenz, W., Strategies for coping with stress. In: Sarason, I., and Spielberger, C. (eds), *Stress and Anxiety*, vol. 2. Washington, D.C.: Hemisphere Press, 1975

Frankl, V., *Man's Search for Meaning*. New York: Washington Square Press, 1963

Glass, D. and Singer, J., *Urban-stress: Experiments in Noise and Social Stressors*. New York: Academic Press, 1972

Heller, K., The effects of sound support: prevention and treatment implications. In: Goldstein, A. and Kanfer, F. (eds), *Maximizing Treatment Gains*. New York: Academic Press, 1979

Henderson, S. and Bostock, T., Coping behaviour: correlates of survival on a raft. *Australian and New Zealand Journal of Psychiatry*, 1975, 9, 221–3

Janis, I., *Psychological Stress: Psychoanalytic and Behavioral Studies of Surgical Patients*. New York: Wiley, 1958

Johnson, J. and Leventhal, H., Effects of accurate expectations and behavioral instructions on reactions during a noxious medical examination. *Journal of Personality and Social Psychology*, 1974, 29, 710–18

Lefcourt, H., Locus of control and coping with life events. In: Staub, E. (ed.), *Personality: Basic Aspects and Current Research*. Englewood Cliffs, New Jersey: Prentice-Hall, 1980

Lundberg, U., Urban commuting: crowdedness and catecholamine excretion. *Journal of Human Stress*, 1976, 2, 26–32

Marmor, J., The psychodynamics of realistic worry. *Psychoanalysis and Social Science*, 1958, 5, 155–63

McGrath, J., *Social and Psychological Factors in Stress*. New York: Holt, Rinehart and Winston, 1970

Mechanic, D., *Students under Stress*. New York: The Free Press, 1962

Seligman, M., *Helplessness: On Depression, Development and Death*. San Francisco: W. H. Freeman, 1975

Shipley, R., Butt, J., Horowitz, E. and Farbry, J., Preparation for a stressful medical procedure: effect of amount of stimulus pre-exposure and coping style. *Journal of Consulting and Clinical Psychology*, 1975, 46, 499–507

Swank, R., Combat exhaustion. *Journal of Nervous and Mental Disease*, 1949, *109*, 475–508

Chapter 6

Jacobson, E., *Progressive Relaxation.* Chicago: University of Chicago Press, 1974

Mahoney, M., *Cognition and Behavior Modification.* Cambridge, Massachusetts: Ballinger Publishing Co., 1974

Meichenbaum, D., *Cognitive Behavior Modification: An Integrative Approach.* New York: Plenum Press, 1977

Wolpe, J., *Psychotherapy by Reciprocal Inhibition.* Stanford: Stanford University Press, 1958

Chapter 7

Averill, J., The factors of grief. In: Izard, C. (ed.), *Emotions and Psychopathology.* New York: Plenum Press, 1979

Ayalon, O., Coping with terrorism: the Israeli case. In: Meichenbaum, D. and Jaremko, M. (eds), *Stress Prevention and Management.* New York: Plenum Press, in press

Bandura, A., Self-efficacy: towards a unifying theory of behavioural change. *Psychological Review*, 1977, *84*, 191–215

Bourne, P., *The Psychology and the Physiology of Stress.* New York: Academic Press, 1969

Cormier, W. and Cormier, L., *Interviewing Strategies for Helpers*. Belmont, California: Wadsworth, 1979

Grinker, R. and Spiegel, H., *Men under Stress*. Philadelphia; Blakiston, 1945

Janis, I. and Mann, L., *Decision Making*. New York: Free Press, 1977

Meichenbaum, D. and Jaremko, M., *Stress Prevention and Management*. New York: Plenum Press, in press

Moos, R., *Evaluating Treatment Environments: A Social Ecological Approach*. New York: Wiley, 1974

Novaco, R., *Anger Control: The Development and Evaluation of an Experimental Treatment*. Lexington, Massachusetts: D. C. Heath, Lexington Books, 1973

Novaco, R., Stress inoculation: a cognitive therapy for anger and its application to a case of depression. *Journal of Consulting and Clinical Psychology*, 1977, 45, 600–8

Novaco, R., A stress-inoculation approach to anger management in the training of law enforcement officers. *American Journal of Community Psychology*, 1977, 5, 327–46

Proshanksy, H., Ittleson, W. and Rivlin, L., *Environmental Psychology: Man and his Physical Setting*. New York: Holt, Rinehart and Winston, 1970

Turk, D., Meichenbaum, D. and Genest, M., *Pain and Behavioral Medicine*. New York: Guildford Press, in press

Index

Green, B. 23–5
Group support 135–8
Guest, D. 53–5
Guntern, G. 25–6

H

Heart disease 49, 50, 53, 56–61, 91, 95
Heart rate 10, 20, 41, 47, 109
Henderson, S. 94
Hiroshima victims 68
Holocaust victims 81
Humour 81, 82, 96, 127

I

Illness 27, 36, 48, 49–52, 65, 69, 78, 80–1, 82, 89, 90,
     91–2, 94, 133
Israeli communities 136

J

Jacobson, E. 100
James, W. 69
Janis, I. 68, 92, 136
Janoff-Bulman, R. 34–7
Johnson, J. 87

K

Kubler-Ross, E. 64–5

L

Lazarus, R. 40–1
Leventhal, H. 87

W

Psychotherapy

For advice on seeking therapy it is always a good idea to consult your own doctor first.

For more information about the ideas, approaches and methods outlined in this series, here are some useful addresses:

British Association of Psychotherapists
121 Hendon Lane, London N3

Institute of Behaviour Therapy
43 Weymouth Street, London W1

MIND (National Association for Mental Health)
22 Harley Street, London W1

Northern MIND
158 Durham Road, Gateshead, Tyne & Wear NE8 4EL

North West MIND
Room 223, Miller House, Miller Arcade, Preston, Lancashire PR1 2QA

Trent MIND
69/71 Wilkinson Street, Sheffield S10 2GJ

Wales MIND
23 St Mary Street, Cardiff CF1 2AA

West Midlands MIND
52/54 Lichfield Street, Wolverhampton WV1 1DG

Yorkshire MIND
155/157 Woodhouse Lane, Leeds LS2 3EF

Many advertisements offering help for specific problems are genuine. Nevertheless it is always advisable to check organizations offering such services with your local Community Health Council (for London the equivalent organization is the Area Health Authority, London). These bodies act as independent watchdogs for local health services. The address of your local Community Health Council will be available from your local Citizen's Advice Bureau.